The Essential Nostradamus

OTHER BOOKS BY JOHN HOGUE

A New Cold War: The Prophecies
of Nostradamus,
Stormberger and Edgar Cayce
Predictions 2015
The Saturn Prophecies: 2013-2042
Nostradamus: The War with Iran
Nostradamus and the Antichrist,
Code Named: Mabus
Messiahs: The Visions and Prophecies
for the Second Coming
The Last Pope: The Decline and
Fall of the Church of Rome
The Millennium Book of Prophecy
Nostradamus: The Complete Prophecies
1000 for 2000 Startling Predictions
for the New Millennium
Nostradamus: The New Millennium
The Last Pope "Revisited"
Nostradamus: A Life and Myth
The Essential Hopi Prophecies
Kamikaze Tomorrowland (a ScryFy Short Story)

The Essential Nostradamus

John Hogue

Acclaim for John Hogue:

"I have known John Hogue for fifteen years. Every year, he predicts on the program [Dreamland] and every year, he proves to be fireproof. He's accurate. Uncannily accurate!"

—**Whitley Strieber**, author of *Communion* and *The Coming Global Superstorm* with Art Bell

THE ESSENTIAL NOSTRADAMUS
Published by John Hogue
Copyright © 11 September 2014 by HogueProphecy Publishing
All rights reserved.

ISBN: 1502840472
ISBN 13: 9781502840479

First Edition © 2002, Vega (a Member of the Chrysalis Books plc.)

Cover design: John Hogue, Gail LaForest
Cover photo of author: Linda Schwartz
(http://www.whidbeyartists.com/schwarz.html)

DEDICATION

To "the Man from the East."

ACKNOWLEDGMENTS

Thanks to my conceptual editor, Francis Perry, my designer, Gail LaForest and my friend and fellow literati, J.R. Rain.

TABLE OF CONTENTS

Introduction:

THE LIFE AND WORKS
OF NOSTRADAMUS

Distilling the Diviner

Nostradamus casts his giant shadow on the world of prophecy as the genre's greatest failure, but not because his 1,477 predictions were wrong. This sixteenth-century doctor, herbalist and Renaissance man accurately foresaw many of the important figures, defining events, and calamities of the last four-and-a-half centuries. He saw the coming of the French and Russian Revolutions. He named Louis Pasteur outright and dated his groundbreaking discoveries in medicine. Nostradamus described men walking on the Moon and falling from the skies in the *Challenger* space shuttle disaster. He saw Napoleon and Hitler, the world wars and the global village that followed with the human race of that far-off time (our time) flying through the air "over mountains, continents and oceans." Nevertheless, he failed in his mission as a prophet because we continue not to heed his warnings.

Perhaps the sheer volume of his 36,000 words of warning tend to overwhelm those who might gain insight and help prevent the dangerous potential events that are coming. Our fast-paced time of fast food and fast facts requires the creation of a book that briefly and comprehensively gives the reader of this travail-full new millennium the essential view of things to come.

ESSENTIAL NOSTRADAMUS will take you through a fundamental examination of the master prophet's life and his magical practices used to see tomorrow. After a short review of the dos and don'ts of decoding Nostradamus' symbolic language, we then plunge through a few dozen of his most chilling and clear prophetic successes. Finally, we make a great leap forward into an indispensable exploration of the nightmares and hopes of the new millennium and beyond.

The Life of Nostradamus

Family Background

Michel de Nostredame was born in 1503 to recently "Christianized" Jews in the town of St. Rémy, Provence, yet scholars still debate over his family's true background and economic status. Some believe he was the son of a Jewish grain dealer called Jaume, while others say his father was a prosperous notary by the name of Jacques.

Michel's mysterious talent for prophecy was first encouraged by both of his grandfathers who took turns being his tutor. They were both learned men of the Renaissance, and were in their younger days the personal physicians to the most free-thinking king of the time, Réné the Good of Provence, and his son, the Duke of Calabria. Their eager pupil, Michel, showed a superior aptitude for mathematics and the celestial science of astrology.

Education
Michel's paternal grandfather deemed him ready at 14 to study liberal arts at Avignon, the papal enclave of Provence. At 19 he was sent to study medicine at the University of Montpellier (although some scholars dispute the timing and believe he spent the following nine years roaming Southwest France, learning directly from life his legendary skills as an herbalist and free-style apothecary). If the former story is correct then our young and gifted medical student breezed through his baccalaureate examinations in 1525. Soon afterwards an outbreak of bubonic plague disrupted his schooling for a few years. Sixteenth-century France suffered from seasonal bouts of *le Charbon*, the figurative description of the day for the carbon-black pustules of the Black Death. So severe was this new outbreak that the University of Montpellier closed its doors, and faculty and students alike fanned out through Southern France to battle the disease. With a license to practice medicine in hand, Michel de Nostredame saddled

up his mule, packed his medical and astrological books and astrolabe, and set off on the open road down the trail of the plague. The emergency had liberated him from the fundamentalist views of his teachers and provided the freedom to put his medical theories to the test.

The Young Plague Doctor

Whatever Nostradamus was by 1525—either a free lance apothecary, or one licensed to practice medicine, if not yet a degreed physician—he followed the plague's shadow westwards through Montpellier, Narbonne, Toulouse, and all the way to Bordeaux, never leaving a town until the danger had passed. He honed his skills and availed himself of the knowledge and teachers of the Counter-Reformation's mystical underground of alchemists, Moorish medicine men, Jewish Cabalists, and pagans. His understanding of the importance of hygiene was considered quite progressive and controversial for the times, given that the doctors of his day seemed to have professional amnesia about the classical fathers of Western medicine such as Hippocrates (460-370 b.c.e.) and Galen (129-c. 200 c.e.) who were staunch believers in hygiene and the importance of clean water sources to sustain health. By 1529 he returned to Montpellier, where he received his doctorate and adopted the Latinized name *Nostradamus.* He remained a professor of medicine there for the following three years until friction over the rigid and conservative curriculum became unbearable and he left to set up a practice in Toulouse.

The Rise and Fall of Dr. Nostradamus

In 1534 he moved to Agen, where he became friends with the volatile Julius-César Scaliger, one of the great minds of the Renaissance. In Agen Nostradamus fell in love with and married Adriète de Loubéjac. Skeptics theorized that sympathetic biographers mistook the name of Nostradamus' bride for that of Scaliger's beautiful 16-year old wife, whose name was Andriète de Roques-Lobéjac. We do know she bore him a beautiful boy and girl, and for the next three years Nostradamus eased into an idyllic family life and a flourishing medical practice.

In 1537, tragedy struck with such brutal intensity that it nearly shattered the young doctor's spiritual and mental health. In that year the plague returned to Agen and his wife and children were among its first victims. Friends and family turned against him, holding him responsible for their deaths. Scaliger, who was prone to violent argument and breaking his friendships, chose this moment to castigate the young doctor. His wife's family sued him for their dead daughter's dowry and won. His patients abandoned him, since their superstition convinced them that a doctor who could not save his own family must be in league with the devil.

Next came the Church authorities questioning chance remarks made years before. He had seen an inept workman making a bronze statue of the Virgin Mary and had commented that he was "casting demons." After receiving the summons to face the Inquisition at Toulouse, Nostradamus packed a few belongings and stole away into the night on his mule.

The Pilgrimage to Prescience

History's account of the next six years of his life is vague and often apocryphal. We know he traveled as far north as Lorraine, as far east as Venice, and lived for a time as far south as Sicily. One can suppose that he wandered through Western and Southern Europe to avoid the Church Inquisitors, while trying to pick up the shattered pieces of his life with a pilgrimage of self-discovery. It is during this dark night of Nostradamus' wandering soul that the first legends of his awakening prophetic powers began to emerge.

A group of Franciscan monks traveling one day along a muddy road near the Italian town of Ancona saw the solitary doctor walking towards them. As they approached he stood aside to let them pass, but on regarding Brother Felice Peretti he immediately bowed, then knelt in the mud before him. The friars, knowing that Peretti had previously been a swineherd and was of lowly birth, were puzzled by this homage and asked

Nostradamus to explain. He replied: "I must yield myself and bend a knee before His Holiness."

The friars chuckled under their cassock hoods at the explanation but, 40 years after his chance meeting and nearly 20 years after the death of Nostradamus, Brother Peretti became Pope Sixtus V.

Another legend chronicles Nostradamus' stay at the château of Lord de Florinville while, on a stroll with his host around the grounds, the conversation turned to prophecy. Florinville wanted to put the prophet's powers to the test. They had stopped before a corral containing two suckling pigs, one black, and one white. When Florinville asked Nostradamus which pig would provide dinner that night, he replied without hesitation, "We will eat the black pig, but a wolf will eat the white."

Florinville secretly ordered his cook to slaughter the white pig. The cook dressed the pig for the spit and left the kitchen on an errand, forgetting to close the door. On his return, he found Florinville's pet wolf cub happily devouring the white pig. The horrified man shooed it away and ran to the corral to fetch the black pig.

At dinner that night all mouths watered as the cook set the roasted pig before Lord Florinville, who smiled at Nostradamus across the table.

"We are not eating the black pig as you have predicted. And no wolf will touch it here."

Nostradamus was so adamant that this was the black pig that Lord Florinville eventually summoned the cook. The cook admitted everything under the penetrating gaze of Nostradamus gray eyes.

The Plague Doctor Returns

Nostradamus returned to South France in 1544, and set up medical practice in Marseilles. In the winter of 1544-45, Provence suffered one of its worst floods on record. By spring the rains and flood waters receded, leaving one of the most devastating pestilences of the century in their wake. Hysteria and death spread over most of Southern France for several years. In 1546, the city fathers of Aix-en-Provence summoned Nostradamus to the afflicted capital of Provence to combat a severe outbreak of *le Charbon*. Nostradamus worked around the clock for the next 270 days ministering to the sick.

With the assistance of an apothecary named Joseph Turel Mercurin, Nostradamus produced fragrant herbal and rose-petal lozenges. He admonished his patients to always keep these "rose pills" under their tongues without swallowing them. Other surviving fragments of his medical journals imply that, as much as possible, he avoided bleeding his plague patients. Nostradamus advised patients to make sure their drinking water and bedding were clean, and to open the windows of their foul-smelling bedrooms to fresh air. He suggested they eat a balanced diet low in animal fat and get a moderate amount of exercise. These regimens of diet, exercise and hygiene, along with his legendary health and fearlessness when facing disease, may have helped more to cure his patients than the rose pills themselves.

Once the danger had passed, the city parliament gave Nostradamus a pension for life and the citizens of Aix showered him with gratitude and awards. It is said that he gave many of the gifts to the families and dependents of those he had not been able to save.

The hero of Aix next received a call for help from the City Fathers of Salon. He had no sooner cured the plague there when he received an urgent call from Lyons. The city records cite him for controlling an outbreak of whooping cough through mass prescriptions filled by one pharmacist named René Hepiliervard.

A New Life
Nostradamus returned to Salon in 1547 to settle there for the rest of his life. He was enchanted by the little town's beauty and dry, sunny skies. He stayed at the house of his brother, Bertrand de Nostredame. Bertrand is purported by some biographers to have introduced Nostradamus to an attractive and intelligent young woman of a wealthy and respected Salonoise family. The untimely death of Jean Baulne would soon make

the widow, Ann Ponsarde Gemelle, the new bride of the middle aged Dr. Nostradamus.

For the next eight years Nostradamus gradually withdrew from medical practice to engage himself in a highly successful cosmetics cottage industry with the help of his wife.

Writing a History of the Future

From 1548 onwards, Dr. Nostradamus plunged wholeheartedly into the occult. He transformed a room in the top floor of his house into a secret study, and by 1550 started publishing an annual almanac that made a few cautious stabs at prediction. He was so encouraged by the reaction to his prophecies that he embarked on an ambitious project: the future history of the world, told in 1,000 enigmatic quatrains (four-line poems), using a mixture of French, Latin, Italian, Hebrew, Arabic and Greek.

Nostradamus began work on *Les Propheties* on the night of Good Friday 1554. The plan was to compose a total of ten volumes, or "Centuries," of one hundred quatrains each.

He published the first three centuries in May 1555. They open with a *Preface* dedicated to his infant son, César. It contained confessions and descriptions of his prophetic techniques and a prose prophecy that stretched his vision all the way to the year 3797 c.e. Nostradamus cranked out Centuries 4 through 7 by 1557. Incomplete editions survive of Century 7. He finished and published the final three Centuries in 1557 and 1558, along with an ambitious letter of prophecies, known as the *Epistle to Henry II*, written in a macabre and psychedelic prose rivaling the *Book of Revelation.* His publisher printed special copies of the Epistle and the last 300 quatrains that found their way to French Court, but it was Nostradamus' wish to delay general publication until after his death to protect his growing family from the mounting popularity and controversy of his prophecies. Nostradamus and Anne would eventually have six children.

Notorious Fame

Queen Catherine de' Medici was among the first people to read Centuries 1 to 3 of *Les Propheties* in the early Summer of 1555, the reason being her love of Occult literature. She had spies in the Royal Library ever on watch for any new tomes on magic and prophecy passing through its process of examining and approving their copyright in the French realm. They no doubt delivered to the queen an early printed copy. De' Medici came to read the quatrain predicting the death of her husband, King Henry II, in a jousting accident. Nostradamus was summoned to Paris to a royal audience with the king and queen to explain himself. He thereafter became an intimate occult friend to Catherine de' Medici. With most royal approval, *Les Propheties* was all the rage at French court. Nostradamus was back in Salon when

Henry II fulfilled that prophecy in 1559. This was the first of several successful predictions fulfilled in his own lifetime that made Nostradamus the talk of the courts of Europe.

Persecution followed fame. During the early 1560s France was lurching towards the first of nine civil wars fought over religion. Though he outwardly practiced Catholicism, many Catholics viewed the Christianized Jew as a Calvinist heretic, while the Protestants and Calvinists of Salon cursed him as a papist.

Greater dangers also attracted greater supporters to his name. The Duke and Duchess of Savoy became his patrons. It is said he cast what became a most accurate astrological natal chart for their newborn son, who later became Savoy's most remarkable ruler, Charles-Emmauel "the Great." It is during this time that Nostradamus played with writing Centuries 11 and 12, but only fragments remain. From 1550 until his death he continued to compose highly popular annual almanacs containing prose prognostications, and later, annual bundles of quatrains predicting the events of the coming year.

Honored in his Final Days
In 1564, while on a tour of Pacification through the French realm, Catherine de' Medici (now the Queen Regent) and the adolescent King Charles IX made a point to visit the aging prophet of

Salon. Before resuming their tour, Catherine had Charles IX honor Nostradamus with the title Counselor and Physician in Ordinary, with the privileges and salary this implied.

Nostradamus reached the high point of his prophetic career with only a year and eight months left to live. His noted robust health underwent a rapid collapse by mid-1566. In June, upon returning from the royal Embassy of Arles as a representative of the king, Nostradamus had a severe attack of gout, which soon developed into dropsy (pulmonary edema). He asked his family and disciples to move his deathbed into his beloved secret study where, in great physical pain, but spiritual serenity, he awaited his end. His last prediction concerned his own approaching death:

On his return from the Embassy, the king's gift put in place. He will do nothing more. He will be gone to God. Close relatives, friends, brothers by blood (will find him) completely dead near the bed and the bench.

At daybreak on 2 July 1566, family and friends found him dead in his bed with his swollen leg propped on a bench, exactly as he predicted.

Anne carried out her husband's final request that his coffin should be standing upright, enclosed within an inside wall of the Church of the Cordeliers of Salon.

Angels, Daemons and Divination

A good magician never reveals the full nature of his secrets. At best we only have Nostradamus' hints at the magical route he took to unlock the future.

Nostradamus' various confessions on the matter hint at his prophetic power coming from God. The mortal prophet received messages carried down through a relay consisting of a hierarchy of spirits. Nostradamus, standing in his magic circle in his secret study, may have used ancient Cabalistic techniques to conjure good angels rather than the more elemental and lower denizens of the astral plane known as *daemons*.

In his prophecies he speaks of divine ones, or angels, that sit at his side when he is deep in trance. They reveal to him what he calls a "prophetic heat" and vision. This divine fire of prophecy descends upon the prophet's stilled mind and heart like the brilliance of the Sun. It guides the spectral emissaries to influence the mortal medium to prophesy.

Nostradamus' Bible of Magic

Nostradamus' occult confessions reveal his heavy reliance on the Neo-Platonist magician Iamblichus (died, 330 c.e.). He no doubt had a copy of Marsilio Ficino's translation of Iamblichus' *De mysteriis*

Aegyptiorum, the bible on Egyptian, Chaldaean and Assyrian magic rituals that is often cited in Nostradamus' confessions about his magic rituals. Nostradamus also relied on the occult works attributed to the biblical King Solomon, and a rare treatise in Greek by the noted Byzantine historian, Michael Psellus (1018-1078), entitled *Of Daemons According to the Dogma of the Greeks.*

Nostradamus' Philosophy on Time

If we take his studies of classical divination as an indicator, it is safe to say that Nostradamus believed that the divine world of eternity contains all the potential destinies, causes and effects, and archetypes expressed in the physical, time-bound world. A mortal man, by nature, is limited to the rules of time and space. His sense of time is linear. He is like a man at the fork of a crossroads who cannot look beyond the horizon of the present to see which road is the right one to travel. But through magical meditations, and with the assistance of divine messengers and lower elemental spirits, he can enter within himself, to access the invisible, latent flame of divinity sleeping within everyone. For brief moments he can tap into the divine ecstasy of the *Ever Now* state of eternity, and from this higher state of awareness, his soul can gaze down at the same crossroads stretching beyond the physical present and see potential future events on various paths of destiny radiating from the present. It is as if these divine spirits, in union with his own expanded consciousness, take him to a much higher vibration from where he can view the faraway bumps and turns down the crossroads of destiny.

How the Prophet Prepared Himself to See the Future

We can surmise that a nocturnal session would see Nostradamus prepare himself by fasting for three days to disconnect from the corporeal energies of the body. He would also abstain from sex to build his psychic energies and direct them upwards towards the ethereal plane. Night is preferable for the conjuration of spirits. The weather should not be stormy, too windy or disturbed by the shadows of moving clouds. A magician must take great care to astrologically plot the right hour for conjuring each specific class of spirit messenger: the archangels, angels, heroes and elemental daemons.

Before entering his secret study he would bathe himself in consecrated water, don a simple robe, and take up a laurel branch as his magic wand. He would enter a consecrated circle drawn in the center of the floor and perhaps illuminated by candles. The circle protected him from the divine emissaries about to be conjured. His writings admit to a preference for angelic and daemonic messengers of fire and their different qualities of divine, nonphysical light, although the works of Iamblichus and King Solomon also describe the invocation of spirits of water, earth, air, and ether. Nostradamus loved the hot and dry climate of his native Provence; perhaps he had his best success with the "fiery missives" of angelic spirits.

Our prophet sits upon a tripod over which a brass bowl is filled to the brim with steaming water made pungent with stimulating oils and perhaps lightly narcotic herbs. This is done to imitate the fumes of a volcanic fissure the priestess of Ancient Greece (known as the Oracle of Delphi) imbibed to prepare for her possession by a god so that she could predict the future. Between deep inhalations of pungent vapor he, like the oracle, chants magic incantations and feels the minute flame of divine fire penetrate his soul. At the right moment, Nostradamus dips his wand, a laurel branch, into the brass bowl. He anoints his foot and the hem of his robe. A sudden rush of paranormal energy into his body is at first frightening, but he surrenders himself to it and ecstasy transports him into a psychic trance. The voice of a higher entity vibrates inside him. Later, he lowers a consecrated pen to parchment and writes a history of the future, as it was told and revealed each night by the hushed voice of his divine messenger.

The Divination Techniques of Nostradamus

Nostradamus' incantations for spirit communication are mostly derived from the *Keys of Solomon*. It is possible he uttered them in Hebrew rather than Latin. The magical tools and disciplines he may have used within the circle to bring himself into a trance were varied, although most of them required the discipline of scrying—gazing on certain objects without blinking. Some believe he sat in his observatory gazing at the reflection of stars in a dark bowl of water. Though Theurgy (conjuring entities from higher planes) was his main practice, he sometimes may have gazed at a flame or peered into the deep and polished surface of a lead or pewter mirror when in the magic circle of his study.

The most famous and controversial Assyrian technique of hydromancy comes from his study of Psellus, who wrote:

> *Thus those about to prophesy take a basin full of water which attracts the spirits creeping stealthily in the depths. The basin then full of water (to the brim) seems...to breathe as with sounds; it seems to me that the water was agitated with circular ripples as from some sound emitted below.*
>
> *Now this water diffused through the basin differs but little in kind from water out of the basin, but yet it much excels it from a virtue imparted on it by the incantations which have rendered it more apt to receive the spirit of prophecy. For this description of spirit is peevish and earth-bound and much under the influence of composite spells.*

When the water begins to lend itself as the vehicle of sound, the spirit also presently gives out a thin, reedy note but devoid of meaning; and close upon that, while the water is undulating, certain weak and peeping sounds whisper forth predictions of the future.

How Nostradamus set down His Visions

At first light he would move from the magic circle over to his writing desk and set to work translating his visions into prose, pulling out consecrated paper to write with a pen made from the third feather of the right wing of a white male gosling, ceremoniously plucked.

Only on the first rewrite would Nostradamus cloak his notes into obscure and coded four-line poems. He made sure the prophecies were out of sequence. Legend states that he wrote each quatrain on a single piece of paper and had Jean-Aymes (Aimé) de Chavigny, his secretary and apprentice, toss them in the air to be gathered in whatever order they fell. Although many Nostradamians down through the centuries want to believe he hid his original notes for later discovery, it is more likely he consigned them to the flames of his alchemical furnace once the quatrains were written.

Astrology Disciplines Used

Judicial Astrology is known today as Political, or Mundane Astrology. It encompasses the plotting of astrology charts for countries, state leaders, and the birth of constitutions and governments. Nostradamus in his writings confesses that he used the discipline of judicial astrology to translate his fanciful visions into objective ideas for writing.

How to Decipher Nostradamus

His writings tell us that Nostradamus consciously chose to write about the future in an obscure and calculatedly nebulous style so that the ignorant and prejudiced would deem him a fool and leave him alone, while the more open minded might pass beyond the verbal roadblocks to glimpse future human potential for good and evil.

Nostradamus establishes some important ground rules:

1. He deals only with significant events that could—or did—change the course of history.

2. All the bad grammar, the enigmas, anagrams, the mix of several languages, the bald-faced absurdities and the general cloudiness of his writing are devices to hide truths from those who want the future to mold itself around their hopes and fears. It may even be done to

hide the prophecies from future tyrants, who might recognize their mistakes in the prophecies, change their decisions and perhaps create a worse future than Nostradamus had foreseen. Imagine what would happen if in 1990 Saddam Hussein had recognized himself in the prophecies and decided to attack Kuwait in 1996 after he tipped his missiles with nuclear weapons? A man who can see tomorrow has a great karmic responsibility not only to illuminate but also to protect the future from evil people.

3. Obscurity works as a pacifier. The mediocre-minded can project their ideas on Nostradamus' opacity and satisfy themselves that he is a charlatan that supports impressionable people projecting their wish-fulfilling sentiments on his cloudy verses.

    Nostradamus hinted that he wrote his special prophetic language for the meek— or better, the "humble"—in spirit, who are willing to move beyond their own conditioned and egoistic projections to experience Nostradamus' hidden secrets.

Before beginning a journey through time and our projections, it would be advisable to study some of Nostradamus' grammar rules and decoding techniques.

Anagrams
Nostradamus scrambled words and phrases to construct other words and phrases using the same letters; for example: *rapis* becomes *Paris*. Nostradamus made his own variations for switching or replacing letters. One or two letters can be dropped; for example, letters can be added and or changed: *Hister* becomes *Hitler*.

No Sequence of Time
The prophecies rarely follow any logical sequence. The events they describe are frequently scrambled out of chronological order—even within a quatrain itself—requiring the interpreter to find key phrases and words linking a telling of events in other verses and piecing the scattered quatrains together into some understandable order.

The Politics of Animal Names
Countries are characterized as animals, in the form of heraldic or mystical symbols associated with a particular country. For example, *Cock* for France, *Bear* for Berlin or Russia, or *Wolf* for Italy.

Proper Names in Uncommon Places
Proper names can be hidden in normal French words and phrases and vice versa. Even verbs and adjectives can hide a name. *Abas* meaning "to put down," can stand for a future candidate for the Antichrist *Mabus*, or for *Abbas*, a common Arabic name.

Insignias as Portents

You will see plays on words and phrases identifying people and movements through their insignias, coats of arms or other emblems.

Remote Viewing

Geographically speaking, the predictions that apply to France and its neighbors are clearer and more numerous than those about distant lands.

Alternative Futures

To the modern reader most of Nostradamus' predictions seem obscure tangles of syntax and jumbled meaning. Of his nearly 1,500 quatrains (if you include the almanacs) over 800 are little more than augury-babble. They may be just his prophetic mistakes, or perhaps some seem nonsensical to us because their details concern events in our unknown future. I believe many of the incomprehensible quatrains are accurate chronicles of events that might have been if history had taken a different turn—predictions for a parallel universe, even.

The Difficulty in Deciphering Nostradamus

Nostradamus intentionally obscured his prophecies, setting the stage for interpreters to attempt untangling them for centuries to come. Whether a given interpretation for a quatrain is the one he intended or whether his wildly obscure crabbed poetry was meant to unlock the interpreter's own second sight cannot be resolved. The obscurity by its nature renders it difficult to prove or disprove that our interpretations of Nostradamus are the correct ones. Sometimes the commentators accurately foresee future events reflected in the prophet's obscurity even when their slant on a prophecy, in my opinion, was not aligned with Nostradamus' intent.

A deep and careful examination of his prophecies will reveal evidence supporting the argument that Nostradamus had many layers of intention for the use of his prophecies. An important one is that each generation can use them to see how the infinite potentials of the future reflect the positive and negative consequences of our present actions. If we can correctly interpret these potentials they can help us change ourselves for the better, *today*, because we can never live in the future. It has always been, and it will always be, *today* where all potentials of the future manifest.

chapter one

Prophecies
From The Past

Nostradamus wrote over a thousand predictions. These are a few examples of
his hundreds of prophetic successes.

The Jeane Dixon of the 16th Century:
Predicting the Death of
Henry II

Le lyon ieune le vieux furmontera,
En champ bellique par fingulier duelle:
Dans caige d'or les yeux luy creuera,
Deux claffes vne, puis mourir, mort cruelle.

The young lion will overcome the older one
On the field of combat in single battle:
He will pierce his eyes through a golden cage
Two wounds made one, then
he dies a cruel death.

1 Q35[1]

[1]Indexing for prophecies taken from Nostradamus' work *Les Propheties*: 1 (Century/Volume) Q (Quatrain number) 35

The quatrain foretelling the death of King Henry II of France in a jousting accident is one of the most famous, pre-documented and successfully fulfilled prophecies in history. It has only one comparable parallel to our time. In the 1950s American Psychic, Jeane Dixon, began documenting accurate forecasts of the rise of John F. Kennedy to the presidency and his assassination.

At the end of June 1559, Henry II ignored all warnings coming from Nostradamus and others against participating in ritual combat and decided to celebrate the dual marriage of his sister Marguerite to the Duke of Savoy, and his daughter Elizabeth by proxy to King Philip II of Spain, by staging a three-day tournament along the rue St. Antoine outside of Paris. On the final day the king, resplendent in full gilded armor and wielding a great lion-decorated shield, had demanded one more unscheduled match with the Gabriel de Lorges, the Comte de Montgomery.

Upon his next charge down the lists a great splinter of ragged wood from Montgomery's lance rammed through the king's gilded visor and he fell mortally wounded.

Both men that day held shields embossed with lions. Montgomery was six years younger than Henry, who was 41. A tournament is a *field of* ritual *single combat*. During the final bout Montgomery failed to drop his lance in time. It shattered, sending a large splinter through the king's gilded visor (*golden cage*). Henry suffered two mortal wounds. One splinter had blinded the king's eye, another had impaled his temple; both had penetrated his brain (*two-wounds made one*). He lingered for 10 agonizing days until infection and fever carried him off (*then he dies a cruel death*).

The French Revolution: The Flight to Varennes

De nuict viendra par la foreft de Reines,
Deux pars vaultorte Herne la pierre blanche:
Le moine noir en gris dedans Varennes,
Efleu cap. caufe tempefte feu, fang tranche.

By night he will come by the forest of Reines,
A married couple, devious route,
Queen white stone:
A monk-king in gray in Varennes,
Elected Cap, causes tempest,
fire, and bloody slicing.

9 Q20

On the night of 20 June 1791, King Louis XVI and the French royal family, disguised as servants of Baroness de Korff, left Paris in a heavy covered carriage on a journey north, heading for the border in a failed attempt to escape the French Revolutionaries.

Over two centuries before this doomed escape attempt and its tragic consequences were played out, Nostradamus had foreseen it all.

This quatrain is startlingly accurate in every detail. Its index number 20 stands for the date of the attempted escape—20 June 1791. The "9" is a play on an upside down "6." The royal family's road to freedom took them past the *forest of Reines*, but poor roads and a lack of replacement horses eventually forced their coach to make a time-consuming detour. *Devious* thus describes a detour, the secrecy and their disguise. Witnesses who reported seeing the pair during their escape described them as a *married couple* and others believed Louis was a *monk*, dressed in the *grey* attire of the Carmelite Order. The town of *Varennes* was the scene of their discovery. *Queen white stone* presents for us in only three words a perfect description of Marie Antoinette's appearance and emotional state: she wore a white dress and some said that shock and distress turned her hair white. *White stone* could be a double-pun alluding to both her hardness of heart towards the lower classes and lack of personal warmth, and to her involvement in a notorious diamond necklace scandal prior to the revolution. *Elected Cap*, is Louis Capet, the commoner's name used by the former supreme ruler Louis XVI when he was made the *elected* monarch of the new constitutional government. His execution (*causes tempest*) sparks a counter-revolution that will be suppressed by the Republicans with the blade of the guillotine (*bloody slicing*).

The Doctor Prophet
Names a Medical Giant

Perdu trouué, caché de ƒi long ƒiecle,
Sera Paƒteur demy Dieu honoré:
Ains que la Lune acheue ƒon grand ƒiecle,
Par autres vents ƒera deshonoré.

The lost thing is found, hid-
den for so many centuries,
Pasteur will be honored as a demi-God:
This happens when the Moon com-
pletes her great cycle,
He will be dishonored by other
rumors as foul as farting.

1 Q25

To combat the plague, Nostradamus may have used medical techniques that some believe were

ahead of his time, though others theorize his pas-
sionate promotion of classical views on hygiene
were neglected by his contemporaries which
made it seem novel. One prophecy in particular
supports the former view and has caused much
speculation whether the sixteenth-century doctor
used his prophetic skills to save lives.

Louis Pasteur's discovery that germs pollute
the atmosphere was one of the greatest mile-
stones in medical history, and contemporaries
called him a *demigod.* Until his theories were
proved beyond doubt, he endured vicious attacks
from influential colleagues in the medical acad-
emies of his time. Nostradamus not only names
Pasteur, but the prophet also correctly dated the
establishment of the *Institute Pasteur.* He achieved
this by reference to the last great lunar cycle in
astrology, which began in 1535 and ended in
1889, the year the institute was created.

A century after his death in 1895, a new
scandal threatened Pasteur's legacy. Princeton
historian Gerald Geison, in his book *The Private
Science of Louis Pasteur,* purports to expose a
self-serving and sloppy scientist hiding behind
this legend of scientific discovery and altru-
ism. Geison's source was a careful reading of
Pasteur's original lab books. Pasteur's notes do
show that he tested his rabies vaccine on a nine-
year-old boy bitten by a rabid dog, as is popu-
larly believed, but they also overturn his public
claim that he had done thorough tests before

making a child his lab rat for experimental treatments. Whether Pasteur will be *dishonored* or Geison's book will be viewed as *foul rumors* is left for the future to decide.

France was Warned of Nazi Invasion, but no one Listened

Pres du grand fleuue, grand foffe, terre egefte,
En quinze pars sera l'eau diuifee:
La cité prinfe, feu, fang, cris conflict mettre,
Et la plus part concerne au collifee.

Near the great river, a vast
trench, earth excavated,
It will be divided by water into
fifteen parts:
The city taken, fire, blood, cries
and battle given,
The greater part involving the col-
lision [of forces].

4 Q80

Before World War II, the French government and its military advisors, steadfastly believed that the great eastern underground network of fortifications, called the Maginot Line, was impregnable. Its very existence led to a false sense of security.

Half the fortifications faced the *great river* Rhine. The Maginot Line was broken in 15 places by rivers. No other defensive trench in history, set on any country's eastern frontier, can claim this feature.

The city in the quatrain is Paris, taken as a result of a sudden collision of battles fought by German panzers who sidestepped the Maginot Line to break through French and British forces in Belgium, then plunge deep into France to seize the exposed French capital.

Et tranflaté pres d'arduenne filue... (5 Q45)
...Qu'il mettra foudres, combien en tel arroy,
Peu & loing puis profond és Hefperiques. (4 Q99)
...Mur d'Orient cherra tonnerre efclaire,
Sept iours aux portes les ennemis à l'heure. (5 Q81)

...Near the forest of the Ardennes. (5 Q45)
...He will launch thunderbolts—
so many and in such an array
Near, and far, then deep into
the West. (4 Q99)
...The wall of the East will fall,
thunder and lightning.
In seven days the enemy directly
at the gates. (5 Q81)

Hitler's panzer armies flank the eastern *wall* of the Maginot Line with lightning thrusts through Belgium and a surprise thunder stroke through the Ardennes. After the British Expeditionary Force was evacuated at Dunkirk, Hitler's *blitzkrieg* (lightning war) turned southwest driving through France. The thrust to Paris took only seven days!

Beftes farouches de faim fleuues tranner,
Plus part du champ encontre Hifter fera.
En caige de fer le grand fera treifner,
Quand rien enfant de Germain obferuera.

Beasts wild with
hunger will cross the rivers,
The greater part of the battle-
field will be against Hister.
Into a cage of iron will the great
one be drawn,
When the child of Germany
observes no law.

2 Q24

Europe's vast rivers became natural obstacles playing a major part in Hister's—or Hitler's—"Fortress Europe" defense plan, especially on the Eastern Front. Titanic Soviet offensives crossed rivers: the Volga (Stalingrad, 1942), the Dnieper (Kiev, 1943), the Danube (Budapest, 1944), the Oder (Berlin, 1945); and on the Western Front British and American offensives cross the Rhine (Arnhem, 1944, and the Battle of the Rhine, 1945). The final line describes the madness that befell Germany under the Third Reich. From its inception, a majority of its children were members of the Hitler Youth, which had as its major goal the re-programming of the minds of German children to become good "barbarians." Hitler made his last stand in Berlin, in the underground Fuehrer Bunker. When it was under construction, and before the concrete was poured, photos of the two-story labyrinth of inter-connected rebars made it appear to be a vast cage of iron. Perhaps Nostradamus' guiding fire angels showed him the great cage where Hitler took his own life before the bunker's completion.

Man will Walk on the Moon
And Fall From the Sky

Dedans le coing de Luna viendra rendre,
Ou fera prins & mis en terre eftrange,
Les fruicts immeurs feront à grand efclandre
Grand vitupere à l'vn grande louange.

He will come to take himself to
the corner of the Moon,
Where he will be taken and placed
on alien land,
The unripe fruit will be the
source of great scandal,
Great blame, to the other great praise.

9 Q65

Nostradamus dared to propose that someday men would be able to walk upon another planet. The last two lines could bring us back down to Earth to the *Challenger* disaster. The American space program was castigated for sending their astronauts on the *unripe fruit* of faulty rocket boosters that were prematurely approved to fit the budget. At the time of the *Challenger* disaster, however, the Soviet space program was running smoothly with the complete support of its government and people (*to the other great praise*). Decades later in the 2010s we witness NASA suffering *great blame* for relinquishing a presence of human space exploration by scrapping the US Space Shuttle without a new generation of vehicles ready to replace it. At the same time, the post-Soviet, Russian Federation sustains (*with great praise*) its human presence in space by supplying US and other international astronauts access to Russian launchpads and spaceship transport to crew and supply the International Space Station along with its own cosmonauts.

D'humain troupeau neuf feront mis à part,
De iugement & confeil feparez:
Leur fort fera diuifé en depart,
Kappa, Thita, Lambda, mors bannis efgarez.

Nine will be set apart from the human flock
Separated from judgment and counsel:
Their fate to be determined on departure.

Kappa [K], **Thita** [TH], **Lambda** [L]
dead, banished and scattered.

1 Q81

On January 28th, 1986, seventy-one seconds after lift-off, the United States space shuttle *Challenger* exploded. In an era when space flight would have been the stuff of fairy tales, Nostradamus makes an uncannily accurate description, apart from a mistake in numbers (nine rather than seven killed).

During the months of investigation following the explosion, the National Aeronautics and Space Administration (NASA) came under close scrutiny. The inquiry revealed flaws in the shuttle itself and in command decision-making (*separated from judgment and counsel*).

The final line, with its riddle of Greek letters could spell out the key player in the *Challenger* scandal: K, TH, L = (TH)io(K)o(L) = Thiokol. This could stand for the rocket manufacturer, Morton Thiokol Inc., which designed and built the faulty solid rocket boosters. In the scandal many company heads and engineers, along with a number of senior NASA officials, were fired (*banished and scattered*), although this might equally represent the debris of the shuttle raining down on the ocean surface after the great explosion.

chapter two

Prophecies
From The Present Day
And The Near Future

One of the greatest popular misunderstandings about the prophecies of Nostradamus is that they foretold the end of the world for July 1999. Well, if you are reading this today you know how wrong that interpretation is. Indeed, Nostradamus foresaw at least another 1,798 years of Earth history—and perhaps thousands of years of extraterrestrial history after that—remaining for humanity beyond 1999. Here are a few of the finest examples of present-day and near future prophecies.

The King of Terror is
Revealed

L'an mil neuf cens nonante neuf sept mois,
Du ciel viendra vn grand Roy d'effrayeur.
Refusciter le grand Roy d'Angolmois.
Auant apres Mars regner par bon heur.

In the year 1999 and seven months,
The great King of Terror will
come from the sky.
He will bring back Genghis Khan.
Before and after Mars rules happily.

10 Q72

Nostradamus' most famous doomsday prediction warns future generations of a *King of Terror*
descending from the skies in July 1999. This holy
terror could be Nostradamus' Third Antichrist who
many interpreters thought would reveal himself in
July 1999, and wage war on Israel or its Western
allies *from the sky*, either with a nuclear missile or
with a jet loaded with plutonium dust or chemical weapons detonated over a city. Since July 1999
came and went without much fanfare the supporters of this interpretation had to wait for July of the
year 2000, because you can also translate the opening line's original French to mean you start counting the seven months at the end of 1999—"...in
the year 1999 *and* seven months"—or, July 2000.

Thus the Antichrist interpretation suffered
strike two when no terrorist attacked in July 2000.
Were the interpreters swinging at a non-existent
prescient pitch?

Line three metaphorically describes the time of
the King of Terror's descent from the skies as the
period when China becomes a superpower to rival
America. It must be remembered that Genghis Khan,

the great Mongol king, united the people of China and the Central Asian steppes into the world's first Sino-Islamic superpower. The vast Islamic western wing of his empire included modern-day Iraq, Iran, Pakistan, and the Central Asian republics of the former Soviet Union, implying that a modern Genghis Khan and China might bring those nations again into its sphere of political and economic influence.

The phrase *before and after Mars rules happily* can be interpreted to mean that the higher occult aspect of Mars, as the god of magic and spiritual transformation, *rules happily* in the new millennium. The rise of China as a superpower to match America could either bring balance and stability to the world or a future world war. It all depends on which aspect we trigger by our actions.

Nostradamus often uses personifications to hide a phenomenon rather than a man, or vice versa. What if the King of Terror is not the Antichrist? Perhaps he or "it" has already come since July 1999 through July 2000 and it is descending from our skies right now and will impact human civilization for the next 27 to 30 years.

The King of Terror is Global Warming.

Starting with the year 1998, through the summer of 1999, the world experienced a dramatic upswing in violent weather and abnormally high temperatures, signifying that our polluting of the atmosphere has so effectively trapped the Sun's heat that record-breaking temperature rises are a sign of things to come. It could be that the terror of a climate losing its natural balance might be the cause of global stresses on food, water, and economic sustainability. It may cause "Mars" to rule "happily" in its lower aspect of war and mayhem in some future conflict between China, the Middle East and America.

What if the King of Terror may actually be some man, some Antichrist descending from the skies? Other prophecies hint of a terror descending out of skies over New York City. The date of "July 1999" may not be what it seems, as we will examine shortly, but a code for another time and fireball event fulfilled in 2001 that changed the world for worse.

A Global Drought Over the Earth's Grain Belts

A quarante huict degré climaterique,
A fin de Cancer fi grande feichereffe:
Poiffon en mer, fleuue, lac cuit hectique,
Bearn, Bigorre par feu ciel en deftreffe.

At a latitude of the forty-eight degrees
At the end of Cancer [July 24th]
so great [is the] **drought.**
Fish in the sea, river and lake boiled hectic,
[Southwest France] **in dis-**
tress from fire in the sky.

5 Q98

The findings are in: the year 1998 was the hottest year on record at the time of publishing this new edition (11 September 2014). Nostradamus may have indicated the year 1998 in the indexing of this quatrain. Afterwards in 1999 through 2001 (having chronicled the warmest winters on record at that time) the ice cap, where scientists and explorers from the past would have usually stood over the North Pole, had melted two years in a row. This was the prelude to a chronic pattern. In the winter of 1999-2000, part of the Antarctic ocean ice shield the size of the American state of Delaware broke up and released tens of thousands of ice shards into the southern oceans. By the time of this book's first edition in 2002, the grain belts and Eastern Seaboard of North America had entered their fourth year since 1998 of the greatest water shortage and drought in a century. A similar affliction befell the grain belts of Siberia and Manchuria, setting 30,000 fires in the former, and dust storms over the latter that blot out the Sun in China's capital, Beijing.

Add to this our artificially produced global warming and Nostradamus warns us against creating a future drought of biblical proportions that will burn a swath across latitude 48 in the Northern Hemisphere. Drawing a line across that latitude on a map, we touch on nearly all the world's chief grain belts. If today's amber oceans of wheat stretching across North America, Southwestern France, the Ukraine, Manchuria, and Russia should revert to prairies and inhospitable steppes in a few decades, a global world war may arise not from religious or political differences but out of nations of the Earth fighting over dwindling food and water resources.

I wrote the last paragraph 12 years ago in 2002. Time has only strengthened the view that 1998 was the banner year, the launching point for a climate shift, because ALL of the hottest years ever recorded have come after 1998. It was the marker year that Nostradamus foresaw as the beginning of the king of "climate" terror's descent. (Moreover, in the year of this second edition, 2014, climatologists expect global average temperatures to rival and transcend records broken in 1998.) The 1998 prophecy indexing—quatrain [*19*]98, coming only a year before his 1999 prediction indicates a double entendre future. As we will see later, the themes of a personified Antichrist tied to climate change is an ongoing theme in his prophecies.

Other Nostradamus Climate Change Predictions

Super-hurricanes and Typhoons

La grand cité d'Occean maritime,
Enuironnee de maretz en criftail:
Dans le folftice hyemal & la prime,
Sera temptee de vent efpouuental.

The great city of the maritime ocean,
Surrounded by a swamp of crystal:
In the winter solstice and the spring,
Will be tried by a terrible wind.

9 Q48

A great city port of the future is described as a *swamp of crystal*. This could be Nostradamus' attempt at picturing the abstract, futuristic architecture of today's crystal, shard-like skyscrapers of Pudong, Shanghai, Hong Kong in China or Brisbane and Sydney, Australia. Even Miami or, for instance, New Orleans surrounded as it is by the swampy Mississippi Delta, could be the victim of a future superhurricane. Dating this visitation on some future winter solstice through the spring tends to track our storms away from America and along the coast of the Far East beset by an unnaturally extended and violent typhoon season, such as was endured in 2013, yet far worse. The terrible winds of a string of supertyphoons will slam into East Asia on some near-future January through early spring time window.

Rain Clouds make War and
Rising Oceans

Par les Sueues & lieux circonuoifins,
Seront en guerre pour caufe des nuees:
Gamp marins locuftes & coufins,
Du Leman fautes feront bien defnuees.

**Through the Swiss and
circumjacent places,
Will they be at war over the issue
of the clouds:
Swarm of marine locusts and insects,
The mistakes of Geneva will
be completely exposed.**

5 Q85

Geneva, Switzerland, the second home of the United Nations, is where diplomats often gather to negotiate solutions to the world's problems. This quatrain would forecast complete failure of world leaders to anticipate and set forth a Climate Change Treaty that would successfully lower carbon emissions and stop global warming. Afterwards follows a "war" over the "issue of the clouds"—torrents of heavy rains falling out of a hotter and wetter atmosphere that, along with melting glaciers, inundates the world in floods and rising oceans. The swarm of marine locusts and insects is Nostradamus' attempt to describe helicopters and drones launched from ships involved in what the CIA also predicted in a leaked memo from 2010, that the future will be wracked with dozens of "climate wars" fought over dwindling supplies of fresh water, food and industrial resources.

The next quatrain continues the tale of ecological apocalypse:

Par les deux teftes, & trois bras feparés,
La cité grande par eaux fera vexee.
Des grands d'entre eux par exile efgarés,
Par tefte perfe Bifance fort preffee.

Separated by two heads, and three arms,
The great city will be vexed by waters.
The great ones among them led
astray in exile,
Byzantium hard pressed by the
leader of Persia.

5 Q86

Line one may describe a Hindu god, or perhaps some Brahma-headed and Shiva-armed military machine. *The great city* perhaps is the teaming megapolis of Mumbai, rather than Paris, the usual subject of "great city" verses. It will be flooded. If the Indian slant is correct, this will be one of many crowded urban victims of oceans rising because glaciers all around the world continue to melt causing sea levels to rise and to inundate Mumbai and other ports and coastal cities of every continent. Even Paris, 85 miles inland down the Seine River, will not escape the oceans ascending beyond their natural coastlines. The City of Lights may suffer floods from the ocean high tides pushing a Seine River, already flooded by monsoon-like downpours, back against the city. We also have references to a war between

Turkey and Iran, as both jockey to seize political and economic power in the new Muslim states of Central Asia that have been forming since the fall of the Soviet Union. A major dispute in any war would be over water rights to sustain populations and agriculture. Although global warming floods the edges of continents it desiccates their heart-lands with sustained, biblically terror-inspiring droughts.

A Global Famine is Coming! You have Been Warned

La grand famine que ie fens approcher,
Souuent tourner, puis eftre vniuerfelle:
Si grande & longue qu'un viendra arracher,
Du bois racine, & l'enfant de mammelle.

**The great famine, which I
sense approaching,
Will often turn** [up in various
places] **then become universal:
It will be so vast and long lasting,
That** [people] **will grab roots from the
trees and children from the breast.**

1 Q67

The twenty-first century has come. Each day, 220,000 to 250,000 people are born, more than 100,000 new motor vehicles hit the road, we destroy more than 180 square miles of tropical rain forest, and an additional 60,000,000 metric tons of carbon dioxide contaminate the air.

The new millennium sees the exploding population ever more enamored with the market-side, high-waste-producing American lifestyle, yet Worldwatch Institute reports our current global technologies, infrastructure, and food sustainability can support a maximum worldwide population of only 2.5 billion living the American Dream. Maybe the "King of Terror" came a little later than expected for July 1999. He is the sixth billionth child, born in October 1999; or, perhaps the seven-billionth child born in October 2011? We will add a billion more ecologically harmful little terrors in 2026. By 2020, China by itself could eat up the world, since it will require *all* the grain exports produced around the world in the year 2000 to feed its children. By 2025, India, its neighbor, will run out of potable water. What will these nuclear powers do about their food and water problems then?

The plagues, famines, and droughts predicted by Nostradamus have already begun and continue to be right on astrological schedule, as I correctly forecast in my first book in 1986. The growing world drought now sees more than half the current seven billion people on Earth suffering from lack of adequate water. Crop yields cannot catch up with the demand of 80 to 90 million new mouths the feed each year. Tensions will rise, as will the threat of war.

L'an que Saturne & Mars efgaux combuſt,
L'air fort feiché, longue traiection:
Par feux fecrets, d'ardeur grand lieu aduſt
Peu pluye, vent chault, guerres, incurſions.

In the year when Saturn and
Mars are equally fiery,
The air is very dry, a long comet:
From hidden fires a great place
burns with heat,
Little rain, hot wind,
wars and raids.

4 Q67

Here we have Nostradamus giving us astrological dates marking the spread of wars as a result of the stresses coming from a global drought and famine in the early twenty-first century. Saturn and Mars are *equally fiery* when they come together in an astrological fire sign—preferably one of those most responsible for wars and raids, Aries or Leo. Many twentieth-century wars and military offensives parallel this aspect. Saturn joined Mars in Aries when Hitler's forces entered Warsaw in late September 1939 triggering World War II. In 1968, the Tet Offensive during the Vietnam conflict started with the conjunction of these planets in Aries.

Mars and Saturn in Leo coincide with catastrophes of civil unrest, such as during the Indian Partition of autumn 1947, when bloody riots and sectarian strife killed over one million Hindus and Moslems. In 1998 the conjunction of Mars and Saturn saw the *hot winds* of global warming coincide with the *wars and raids* during Serbia's ethnic cleansing of its Muslim citizens in Kosovo and NATO's air attacks on Serbia.

Mars and Saturn will be equally fiery in Sagittarius twice in the year 2016. Retrogrades of both planets make the next rare and unusually magnified interlude of equal fire signs of war begin from March through May 2016 and again from August through September 2016! The signs point to an intensification of a Second Cold War in the flashpoints of Ukraine and Syria while on another front a war could erupt pitting the US and its Middle Eastern proxies, Israel, Saudi Arabia and the Gulf States, against Iran that ends with catastrophic consequences.

Nevertheless, there are yet other significant fiery transits of Mars with Saturn in Aries in 2026, and again in 2028. At that time the stresses of global warming and population may derail the human race in over 70 regional and civil wars.

9-11
The Attack on the *Hollow Mountains* Of New York

Cinq & quarante degrés ciel bruflera,
Feu approcher de la grand cité neufue,
Inftant grand flamme efparfe fautera,
Quand on voudra des Normans faire preuue.

At forty-five degrees latitude,
the sky will burn,
Fire approaches the great new city,
Immediately a huge, scattered
flame leaps up,
When they want to have verification
from the Normans [the French].

6 Q97

The events of 11 September 2001 peel the nebulous veil off two tragic prophecies that will forever stand as Nostradamus' first successes foretelling events from our new millennium. *New* York *city* is near latitude 45 degrees. It did not exist in Nostradamus' time, and his use of *nouveau* often points to prophecies about a great and "new" Western nation of the future (also called "Americh" in his prophecies), that will include great new cities grasping at tomorrow's skies with towers he called "hollow mountains." New York's correct latitude is between 40 and 41 degrees. One might say Nostradamus got his calculations wrong. There are over 650 references to geographic locations in his prophecies, implying that he had a passion for mapping out the locales of the future. Looking at maps of his day, he was plotting the future's geography without longitude lines. The latitude lines of sixteenth-century maps were a few degrees off true line. On the other hand, it may not be a mistake if he foresaw the great and smoking wound left in the North Tower of the World Trade Center by the impact of the hijacked Boeing 767 passenger jet. Look for yourself at those unforgettable first pictures. The angle of the first jet's mortal thrust was at 45 degrees! The second jet's impact into the South Tower? Also, exactly, forty-five degrees!

Lines two and three describe the flaming engines of both commandeered jet airliners approaching the great new city. They crash into the World Trade Center towers, sending fire-balls of *scattered flame* larger than the entire town in which Nostradamus wrote this prophecy 445 years before.

The last line is the key. You will know a future terrorist attack on New York City has come, when the victims are asking the French to verify that an attack is at hand. There are a number of reports coming from credible news sources, such as the Associated Press and the French newspaper, *Le Figaro*, that prove without a doubt that on 10 September French intelligence sources did warn their American opposites that al-Qaeda terrorists were on the move and American assets in Europe and the United States were threatened by immediate attack. The following morning saw American intelligence officers in Washington, D.C. violently interrupted from their feverish efforts to verify the French claims by one of four airliners hijacked by al-Qaeda terrorists, crashing into the Pentagon. Finally, even the quatrain indexing hides what could be a dating. As we will see later, the attack of the "King of terror"—the man who Nostradamus calls "the Third Antichrist"—comes shortly after the passing of a great comet. The quatrain's indexing of "97" may stand for the passing of Comet Hale-Bopp in 1997.

A second prophecy narrows the focus on New York as Nostradamus' intended "new city" under attack:

> *Iardin du monde aupres du cité neufue,*
> *Dans le chemin des montaignes cauees:*
> *Sera faifi & plongé dans la Cuue,*
> *Beuuant par force eaux foulfre enuenimees.*

Garden of the world near the new city,
In the path of the hollow mountains:
It will be seized and plunged
into a boiling Cauldron,
Drinking by force the waters
poisoned by sulfur.

10 Q49

If you were to stand on the western shore of the Hudson River, in New Jersey (also known as the "Garden State"), and look across to Manhattan Island, you would see the man-made "mountains" of the "world" Trade Center in New York City. Imagine a sixteenth-century man's awe when he beholds two towers with 110 acre-sized stories apiece climbing ten times higher than the highest cathedrals of his day. Would you not call such impossible monoliths, with 50,000 workers teaming inside, *hollow mountains*? Even New Yorkers describe their boulevards among the angular stone and steel crags of their skyscrapers as "canyons." If you wished to reach these twin Everests by rapid transit, it seems the prophet himself has directed you to use the "Path" subway. He calls it as much, using the French equivalent *chemin.* In fact, the second hijacked jet roared across the *Garden* State, casting its shadow over waters of the Hudson that cover the very same "Path" subway tunnel *in the path of the hollow mountains.*

After being stabbed from the air, the hollow mountains are "seized and plunged" into the boiling "vat" or *cuue* (spelled cuve in Modern French) as Nostradamus describes it in Renaissance French. Previous translations have relied on the secondary meaning of *cuve* as a "tub" or "tank." Perhaps Nostradamus, ever the word player, intended more than one of the word's meanings. It must be remembered that before construction crews erected the great towers of the World Trade Center they placed their seven-subterranean floors into a water-tight basement and rectangular sea wall so that the waters of the Hudson River would never penetrate the complex and flood Manhattan's underground subway system. The architects and construction workers affectionately called this watertight foundation "the bath *tub.*"

The primary definition of *cuve* is a ferment-ing cauldron; wherein, Nostradamus, a physician and cosmetics manufacturer by profession, would plunge materials for the mixing of his medicines and cosmetics. The cauldron would summon boiling clouds of steam as objects were seized and thrown into it. The use of *cuve* is a poetic attempt to capture the vision of the vast and mortally wounded World Trade towers plunging to earth from their own weight, into the ferment of boiling clouds made of their own pulverized debris. The last line may describe the toxicity of the debris cloud that blan-keted New York City with the stench of numerous toxic materials including ample levels of asbestos dust. Deep seated fires underneath the hills of debris burned and steamed, cauldron-like, for months.

The final line may also portray a future avoided. If the collapse of the towers had undermined the "tub," the Hudson would have poured into the New York subway system. New York port and civic authori-ties were initially alarmed that the walls might have been compromised and sent teams into the ruined Path subway tunnel at the approaches of the devasta-tion to check for signs of water. None fortunately was found; otherwise, the terrorist attack on *the great new city* of New York might have added tens of thousands of unsuspecting victims, caught in the flooding tunnels after they had overcrowded the subway stations because they were looking for a way to escape Manhattan Island after the attack began. They would have suddenly found themselves forced to drink a wave of poisoned floodwaters, laced, as it were, with the *sulfur,* of toxic debris from the World Trade Center towers.

This final line of Century 10 Quatrain 49 could also augur a future and far more catastrophic attack on New York. I sent my first warnings to my readers about the prophecy of an attack on New York's financial district as far back as 1983. In early 1996, my interpretation was dramatized on national US television for a Fox Network documentary entitled *Prophecies of the Millennium.* While quoting the two prophecies above, the documentary pictured the World Trade Center vanishing in a fireball after which a mushroom cloud looms from the crater that was once the southern "hollow mountain" range of Manhattan Island. I pray that the line *drinking by force the waters poisoned by sulfur* is a failed prophecy of what could be, rather than the next catastrophe waiting to be. Let us hope that the poisoned and sulfuric waters will never come from the detonation of an atomic device in the bilges of an unsuspected cargo ship in New York harbor. If New Yorkers are vigilant, this catastrophe will not occur.

The potential of such an event is implied elsewhere by a respected seer of the last century. America's Edgar Cayce once described a waking dream where he was taken forward to the year 2100. Apparently, two bald and bespectacled scientists of that day, possessing unusually long beards, had "discovered" Cayce in his future reincarnation.

They took him on a tour over America in an anti-gravity, cigar-shaped flying machine. The world had suffered some vast natural disaster a century or so before. Some shift in the continents had made Nebraska—the place from which the ZZ-Top scientists of the future plucked Cayce—into West Coast beachfront property. Later the trio flew over what remained of the ruins of New York, which at the time was undergoing the first stages of a reconstruction. Cayce could not tell whether New York had been destroyed by a natural calamity or by an attack.

In other readings held in a trance state Cayce had predicted a shift of the Earth's axis for sometime shortly after 1998. It has not happened. Nebraska remains a haven for grain harvesters and not beachcombers. At the time of writing the second edition (September 2014), the hollow mountains of New York, including the near-completed World Trade Center One Tower resurrected from the rubble of the World Trade Towers, stands in the tub, defiant against the prophecy of Cayce and my alternative interpretation for Nostradamus' vision. May the new tower ever endure.

The King of Terror as Man and Antichrist

L'an mil neuf cens nonante neuf sept mois,
Du ciel viendra vn grand Roy d'effrayeur.

Refufciter le grand Roy d'Angolmois.
Auant apres Mars regner par bon heur.

In the year 1999 and seven months,
The great King of Terror will
come from the sky.
He will bring back the Khan
of the Mongols.
Before and after Mars rules
happily.

10 Q72

From evil gas of global warming to evil made flesh goes another line of interpretive thinking in this most specific date logged by Nostradamus for our present era.

The first line of 10 Q72, if we translate it exactly from the archaic sixteenth-century French, reads: *L'an mil neuf cens nonante neuf fept mois* (literally: *In the year one thousand nine hundred ninety-nine seven months*). Translators tend to insert the "and" to the line for clarity.

The word *sept* derives from *September*, or *seventh month*. Ever seek to decode Nostradamus armed with a knowledge of classical metaphors so en vogue in France during the High Renaissance. Remember, therefore, that September in Ancient Roman times was once the "seventh" month and not the "ninth" month until the Roman Emperor Julius Caesar and his heir, Octavian Augustus Caesar, had the imperial hubris to manufacture the new months of July and August honoring their egos.

Consider then a new variation intended for the first line: "In the year 1999 September (ninth) month."

Since no terrorist attack on New York happened in September 1999, perhaps even the year is hiding an encoded message. What if we have a rare instance of Nostradamus making an anagram out of a number?

Nostradamus, ever one to be consistently random and chaotic of intuitive mind, would not miss a chance to hide something in a date. The test of truth is that which works. Reverse the numbers in 1999:

$$1999 = 9111$$

Do you see what I see?

In the year 9.11.1 September month
The great King of Terror will
come from the sky.

The date of the 9-11 attacks may be intended. Thus the great King of Terror may be the one who launched the attack, Usama bin Laden, the founder of the jihadist network al-Qaeda. From this age-changing event, came our current times overshadowed by a kind of Cold War on Islamo-fascist terrorists. The United States has seen much of its treasure and esteemed standing in the world drained and harmed as it unilaterally waged war in Afghanistan and Iraq, losing both wars, it would seem. The Middle East is worse for wear and was made more unstable as consequence. The forces of al-Qaeda have now metastasized into the heartland of the Arab states of the Middle East and turned into a more virulent Islamo-Fascist cancer called IS (Islamic State) currently gobbling up large areas of Syria and Iraq in a terrorist Caliphate the size of Great Britain and growing. The region where global civilization draws most of its crude oil has become in the wake of these failed US military adventures a most unstable area and is primed for even greater wars to come from the sectarian civil strife spreading out of Syria, back into Iraq. Iran and Saudi Arabia spar for regional dominance, both potentially starting a nuclear arms race, adding their arsenals to that already existing in Israel, soon making the Middle East ripe for biblical fires of the final battle of Armageddon, it would seem.

This King of Terror, if it is Usama bin Laden only, is he just one of the five figures Nostradamus intends as his chief candidates for his "Third Antichrist," is something we will examine a little later. Whoever he is, follow the sixteenth-century metaphors that unlock the other lines of this prophecy.

This King of Terror will *bring back* Genghis Khan, the *King* (Khan) *of the Mongols*. Nostradamus here is using a historical trauma of Mongol hordes galloping out of Asia that sixteenth-century Europeans of his day still feared might return. He is hinting at a modern context, the rise of China as a superpower, with a stake in the Middle East because, like the old Mongol super-power of the 1300s, this new Chinese hegemon of the twenty-first century, economically at least, extends its empire deep into Islamic states at the threshold of Europe. Iran is China's number one supplier of crude oil and it has taken Iran's side against the West.

The final line is a riddle: *Before and after, Mars rules happily.*

Our detective work must move from sixteenth-century metaphors to the layered symbolism of astrology as Nostradamus would have understood it, classically. At face value, Mars is symbolic of war thriving happily. Yet, the higher aspect of Mars is the *Magus*—the enlightened master and forger of new consciousness, new enterprises and explorations.

Peel the onion of classical allusions further. The term *Magus* was originally applied to high priests of ancient Persia (Iran). Thus he could be saying the modern Islamic Republic of Iran is Mars-Magus "ruling happily" through wars of the Third Antichrist.

A future "Mongol king" (read: a chairman of the politburo of a New China) is Iran's ally. He is that new "Khan" among totalitarian rulers of the awakening capitalist-communist hybrid superpower, The People's Republic of China.

Magus in Mars ruling happily may even imply a code name for Nostradamus' Third Antichrist, our contemporary. If you take the *g* of *Magus*, turn it over, you have *b* for spelling Nostradamus' code name for the Antichrist: *Mabus*.

Mabus The *Third* Antichrist And His 27-Year War

At the time of this writing, no one has yet positively identified Nostradamus' Third Antichrist. In contrast to his certainty about Napoleon and Hitler (called *Napaulon Roy*—Napoleon King— and *Hister* respectively), Nostradamus is less clear who *Mabus*, the third tyrant, is. Perhaps this is an example of his prophetic myopia that enabled him to be clearest about events of local or European history. The prophet's vision tends to be cloudier when it contemplates future events in more distant lands. What does come through clearly is that this third and final Antichrist is not a prominent European leader. He may even be some obscure future terrorist who will trigger World War III with a weapon of mass destruction if we do not identify and restrain him in time.

The following three prophecies give clues for recognizing the third, and last, Antichrist as a contemporary of our times. The first quatrain suggests his base of operations, his nationality and the place in Europe most vulnerable to his attack.

Vn qui les dieux d'Annibal infernaux,
Fera renaiftre, effrayeur des humains:
Oncq' plus d'horreur ne plus dire iournaulx,
Qu'auint viendra par Babel aux Romains.

One who the infernal gods of
Hannibal [Thurbo Majus],
Will cause to be born, terror to all humans:
Never more horror nor the newspa-
pers tell of worse in the past,
Then will come to the Italians
through Babel.

2 Q30

Nostradamus hides the locale of his candidate antichrist number three in the name of the *gods* honored by Punic and Phoenician peoples, such as Hannibal. They were "Baal" worshippers. Each region gave their Baal (Lord) God a personalized name. The Carthaginians called theirs "Baal Hammon." Nostradamus, the Christianized Jew, may be putting into play a pun of "Hammon" and the derisive "Mammon" to indicate his pro-Judeo-Christian bias against the final Antichrist.

In addition, if you look at a modern map of regions marking the extent of Baal worship, you will see that it covers an area that today includes Tunisia, Libya, Palestine, Lebanon, Israel, Iraq, and Syria.

The Romans had a custom of adopting the patron gods of a conquered nation and renaming them in Latin. After the Romans had sacked the city of Carthage at the close of the Third Punic War in 146 b.c.e., they build their own city over its ashes and renamed its god Thurbo Majus. The enigmatic name M-A-*B*-U-S may stand as a classic anagram for "M-A-*J*-U-S."

What do the present-day ruins of an ancient city of Romanized, Baal Hammon worshippers have to do with the Third Antichrist? For one thing, it may indicate the importance of modern-day Tunisia as a base of operations for someone who would later earn the mantle *effrayeur* (terror) to all mankind. The ruins of Carthage are a few miles away from what once had been the chief headquarters and training camp for the PLO (the Palestine Liberation Organization). In the headquarters' heyday during the seventies and early eighties, many figures who have been regarded as radicals in the Palestinian freedom movement learned their infernal trade of terrorism just next door to the ruins of Thurbo Majus. Many of these men and their sons continue their quest in the new millennium to destroy Israel and establish a Palestinian state over its ashes from new bases in places once under the spiritual dominion of the Baal Gods of Hannibal: Lebanon, the West Bank, Jordan, Syria, and Iraq (*Babel*).

The idea of newspapers was unknown in the time of Nostradamus. This fact makes it clear to anyone reading today's newspaper stories about Saddam Hussein, Abu Amar (better known as Yasser Arafat) Abu Nidal or Muammar Qaddafi, or the bombing of the New York Trade Center, that these clues have contemporary relevance. It also strongly implies that:

1.) The next Antichrist after Napoleon and Hitler is from, or based in, North Africa or the Near East.

2.) His weapon is terrorism.

3.) The final line of 2 Q30 implies a horrendous and yet-unseen act of infamy coming either directly from, or supported by *Babel* (modern-day Iraq). A number of extreme Palestinian factions once had their offices in Baghdad in Saddam Hussein's Iraq. Palestinian as well as many other Muslim Sunni jihadists are now rallying inside Iraq to the black banners of ISIS (the Islamic State of Iraq and Syria). In the future, their chief target in Europe will be Italy.

The second quatrain gives us leads to decode the Third Antichrist's name, describe his act of horror and record the vengeance of the devastating counterstroke—all to take place on, or shortly after, the significant transit of a great comet across our skies.

Mabus puis toft alors mourra, viendra,
De gens & beftes vne horrible defaite:
Puis tout à coup la vengeance on verra,
Cent, main, foif, faim, quand courra la comete.

Mabus [Majus] **will soon die,**
then will come,
A horrible undoing of people and animals,
At once one will see vengeance,
One-hundred powers, thirst, fam-
ine, when the comet will pass.

2 Q62

From "Majus" we link to the *Mabus* prophecy of 2 Q62 as the same man. Unlike the first Antichrist, code named PAU, NAY, LORON (Napaulon Roy—Napoleon King) and the second, Hister (Hitler), Mabus is the first casualty of his war and his death triggers an apocalyptic series of events, chief of which is what sounds like the unhinging of the human and animal worlds. In 2008, I described at length the ways that the old French application of the word *defaite* (undoing) could have been intended:

> *This phrase is significant and unique in all of Nostradamus' lurid and violent visions. This "undoing" is huge. Global. The old French for "undoing"* (defaite) *incorporates an event that* undoes, unmakes, unravels *the world of people and animals. It implies a dramatic, sudden and catastrophic defeat, a rout, an eclipse of an age—it decries the fall of shadows over civilization due to the death of Mabus. The horrible undoing is a great wasting, an obscuring of reason, something fundamentally embarrassing to what was perceived as reality, truth, moral, or human before Mabus fell.* Defaite *implies something that emaciates, discomposes civil order and perhaps even unravels the climate and ecological balance, leading to a threat of extinction that in a worst-case scenario decimates the world of people and animals.*
>
> *There might be coming a destruction of people and animals that begins as a military incident or war comes from an ecological disaster and/or global famine and droughts. Or the unraveling has a social-economic trigger, such as the collapse of one or many supersystems that keep our global society functioning. Futurist Roberto Vacca coined and defined the word* supersystem *as super-organizations sustained by machines and single energy sources. For*

instance, our fossil fuel based oil and coal-fired civilization uses the petrochemical supersystem. Agriculture is another system, as is transportation of goods by air, land and sea.

Supersystems are interdependent. The collapse of the GPS satellite system, the internet, information retrieval or the malfunction of any single supersystem can "undo" and unravel the world of humanity, triggering horrible and widespread civil disorder, economic collapse, wars, terrorism, pandemics and famines. In the Epistle *Nostradamus warns that as many as two out of every three people on Earth may not survive the apocalypse after the death of Mabus—that means, in today's numbers, nearly 4.4 billion are carried off.*

To my modern sensibilities it sounds like Nostradamus is describing Mabus as some terrorist who manages to unleash a chemical, biological plague or nuclear attack—or all three. He initiates a war that unravels human commerce and civilization. Perhaps Mabus dies in the attack, a martyr to his cause.

With that said. Remember. Nostradamus is trying to grasp a terrible vision from his sixteenth-century understanding. It might not be what we've posited from our twenty-first-century point of view.

Nostradamus and the Antichrist, Chapter 3: Mabus

The closing lines of the Mabus prophecy of Century 2 Quatrain 62, imply an overwhelming counterattack: *At once one will see vengeance* coming from *one-hundred powers*. The US coalition formed after 11 September 2001 against a perceived global terrorist network numbered around one hundred nations.

The mention of *thirst* and *famine* are common in what one could call Nostradamus' numerous Third World War prophecies taking up the compounding theme of climate change stresses leading to economic collapse and war. You will know such a war is near when there is a global plague of droughts and famines. They exist today, and they are growing from the continued stress placed on the food, water and ecosystems by an unrepentant and inexorable overabundance of people demanding their generous share of less. The final phrase (*when the comet will pass* or *run*) is either literally a portend of a significant comet event taking place at the time of the death of Mabus, or it is metaphorically describing the weapon of his death: a flaming-tailed missile.

The third prophecy ties Mabus as the Third Antichrist and expands on just what his *horrible undoing of people and animals* might be like.

> *L'antechrift trois bien toft annichiliez,*
> *Vingt & fept ans fang durera fa guerre:*
> *Les heretiques morts, captifs, exilez,*
> *Sang corps humain eau rogie grefler terre.*

The Third Antichrist very soon annihilated,
Twenty-seven years his bloody war will last.
The heretics [are] dead, captives exiled,
Blood-soaked human bodies, and a red-
dened, icy hail covering the earth.

8 Q77

We notice the word link to the verse naming Mabus in the similar theme of the first lines in both prophecies. Where 2 Q62 submits that *Mabus will soon die*, the second prediction slightly alters the phrase, saying the Third Antichrist is *very soon annihilated*. Once he dies the first prophecy adds, *Then will come a horrible undoing of people and animals*. The second is gruesomely specific about the dead and the dying. They are soaked and stained red by icy hail showers covering the entire Earth.

Nostradamus is a man of the Renaissance period. He could find it hard to explain a future plague raining from biological and chemical agents. A *terrible undoing of people and animals* could hint to a weapon that unleashes poisons or plagues that can extinguish both animals and humans. To him the scene of *blood-soaked human bodies* under *a reddened, icy hail* may be his attempt to understand and communicate a vision of a chemical or biological attack using a hemorrhagic fever weapon.

Take for instance the Kurdish victims piled in the streets of Halabja, Iraq, a city gassed by

Saddam Hussein's Republican Guards with artillery air busts detonated over their heads. Witnesses said the weapons unleashed clouds of reddish and milky agents staining their human and animal victims with red and white milky droplets. Thus, a milky rain in our future that kills both human beings and animals alike can come from a metaphorical hail shower of chemical or biological vapors; or, fall from the sky in a reddish black rain laced with radioactive fallout such as that seen at Hiroshima.

Nostradamus' open-ended application of *terre* (earth) could have either a local or global use. Is this a description of some climatic catastrophe coming from a detonation of nuclear weapons? If so, then a *reddened, icy hail covering the earth* is a watered down version of a nuclear winter; or, it is a slightly nicer meteorological doom: nuclear autumn. Dust from atomic fire clouds could cool down the climate after a sustained nuclear attack. A little later we will examine how a war of the Antichrist spreading across the Middle East may act as a catalyst for a thermonuclear exchange between Russia and the United States.

The "Third Antichrist" prophecy of Century 8 Quatrain 77 could label the shadowy minions of Mabus as *heretics.* They are terrorists who submit to a religiously extreme and apocalyptic aberration of Islam such as al-Qaeda, or they number as grim, black hooded disciples of an even more

barbaric and fearsome band of holy warriors
called ISIS.

To whichever holy war in the hood they
belong, the prophecy points to their eventual
capture, exile and death. One may already see
the first of these Near Eastern exiles sitting
blindfolded in their red jail jumper suits at camp
X-ray—the US concentration camp established at
Guantanamo Bay, Cuba.

Decoding Names
of Candidates for
Antichrist

I have followed the etymological trail for decades,
trying to uncover clues to just what Nostradamus
meant by the name Mabus. I still believe that the
weight of his interests and prejudices pull the
divining rod of possibility towards the magnetic
hotbed of Middle Eastern and North Africa des-
pots. Today's Arab and Iranian terrorists and mis-
guided zealots are our prime suspects. For me the
Mabus mug shot is flashed upon the film of my
curiosity by Nostradamus' favored mind-melding
"camera" of classical metaphors. In other words,
I have seen him too often color his prophecies in
the cellphone camera-clicked moment of ancient
Greek and Roman images of the future. If the
ancient Romans called the Danube "Hister,"
Nostradamus would hide his Second Antichrist's
name behind that classical Roman label. He

would cloak a vision of a child dreaming his diabolical dreams while resting on the banks of the "Hister" and hide the name of the young Adolf "Hitler."

A study of the last two antichrists indicates that most of the letters needed to decode the name of the Third Antichrist could be found in his enigmatic name. In this way, if Nostradamus is being consistent then we should find the name of the next and final antichrist virtually hiding in the letters M-A-B-U-S.

One terrorist leader caught in US cross-hairs in 2003, then captured and hanged at the end of 2006 could be found by reversing the letters "mabus" to "subam" then reverse any letters again, such as a "b" into a "d" to get "sudam." Nostradamus had knowledge of Arabic, so the phonetic pronunciation of *Suh*-dam is covered. The laws of anagramming Nostradamus applied give us the freedom to replace one vowel "u" with an "a" to get "Sadam." The law of eliminating or adding redundancies to letters allows one to double our "d" to get "Saddam" Hussein.

Play the same game with the founder of the al-Qaeda terrorist organization, Osama bin Laden. First, pronounce the Arabic correctly as Nostradamus would have. Osama is *ooh*-sama or Usama. You can find that u-s-a-m-a + b(in) has nearly all the fixings to cook Nostradamus' code name: "Maaus + b." You need not take the "b" from "bin" Laden to replace one redundant "a," but if you wish you can take the "b" and get "Maabus" then cut the redundant "a" to get "Mabus."

There are many readers during the two terms of President G.W. Bush who believed that only the country with the preeminent arsenal of weapons of mass destruction (the United States to be exact) could cause "a terrible undoing of people and animals" coming from their counterattack on those who might cause their anti-Christian leader to fall early in the conflict. To these interpreters of Nostradamus, Bush was their "Mabus."

Did the idea wash?

Maybe.

The laws of anagram will allow one perchance to rotate letters 180 degrees in lower case. Reverse the sequence of the letters *ma* of "Mabus" (*am*) and turn them upside down and you get *gw*. The "h" in Latin is silent, thus the result is "gw Bus(h)" for (G)eorge (W)alker Bush.

Personally, I did not subscribe to this theory. People leaning politically to the left would argue with some efficacy that President Bush's unilateral and often dictatorial foreign policies, painting over the gray and complex issues with often simplistic, black and white "them or us" brush strokes, might contribute to a climate of global terrorism, but that did not mean he is the man Nostradamus tagged as "Mabus." Still, for the record, I cannot rule out that I may be in error in my view that Mabus and the Third Antichrist are one person. It could be possible that 2 Q62 and 8 Q77 are describing Mabus and the Third Antichrist as two figures pitted at war with each other. However, if this is in fact Nostradamus' intent, then both combatants will be early casualties in their war of wills.

Certainly, even a prophet can mistake two leaders who are bound together by a shared dark destiny as one antichrist, when viewing a far off future. Perhaps he has mistaken them for two sides of the same coin of evil.

The court of future history and events will be the final judge.

If the interpretations presented here are correct then the criterion the future will use to reach that judgment depends of the fulfillment of the following events:

1.) Whoever Mabus is, he is one of the first to fall in the war he launches, be it a war on America or an American instigated war on terrorism.

2.) His death will create a war cry for revenge and there will be a devastating counterattack.

3.) The reaction to his martyrdom and the counterattack will set in motion a 27-year war that first sees terrorism as its opening stage but could eventually escalate and widen its theater of destruction to include an exchange of nuclear, biological and chemical weapons between a number of nations. Whether the unraveling of civilization and the natural world represented by people and animals are either the result of this war or climate change as a *casus belli* is unclear. The worst-case scenario would see the death of the Antichrist somehow drag Russia and America into a thermonuclear war, as further prophecies below indicate. It could be fought over food and other resources in the 2020s. In other words, World War Three becomes a world war *free for all* as nature and civil activity both begin unraveling.

Now let us examine the top candidates for Mabus:

Abu Mazen
(Mahmoud Abbas)
Abu = (M)abu(s) = Mabus
Abbas = (M)abbas = Mabus

The Chairman of the Palestinian Authority, Mahmoud Abbas, whose Palestinian Liberation Organization pseudonym is Abu Mazen, is just one of many Palestinian and other Arab jihadi leaders who are called "Abu" (Father) by their followers and holy warriors. Nostradamians ponder whether the violent death of this Palestinian leader in the near future might knell the death of all attempts to make peace with the Israelis and thus start the 27-year war of the Third Antichrist. Few of the other clues implicate Abbas clearly as a front running candidate.

Saddam Hussein
Saddam Hussein = maddas =
sadam = subam = Mabus

At the time of this writing, no other candidate has apparently fulfilled so many of the clues set in the three quatrains about the Third Antichrist. Beyond decoding his name out of Mabus:

2 Q30: Saddam is from *Babel* (modern Iraq) an area where Baal gods were worshipped. He used terror weapons on his people and he was the talk of newspapers all over the world during his reign. Part of the ruins of Babel (Babylon) were rebuilt with one out of every 100 bricks inscribed with his name in an attempt to cheat time and future ruin.

2 Q62: After Saddam was hung at the end of 2006, Iraq descended into sectarian civil war and the bloodiest years of the US occupation. With the American departure came a further unraveling of, and wholesale slaughter in, Iraq by the invasion of ISIS from Syria. A comet "did" run, one of the brightest comets in 60 years appeared to the naked eye EXACTLY on Saddam Hussein's final night vigil on Earth before his hanging just before dawn on 30 December 2006.

8 Q77: Most of Saddam's henchmen are dead heretics, executed or exiled. The reference to his use of chemical weapons at Halabja (1988) and on the Iranian Army during the Iran-Iraq War

(1980-1988) is implied. Saddam Hussein became President of Iraq and its dictator on 16 July 1979. He waged perpetual internal warfare with Iraqi Kurdish or Shia citizens or with his external neighbors for the 24 years he was in power and wars raged for another three years during his incarceration. He was hanged by the neck in the 27th year after he came to power! (*The Third Antichrist very soon annihilated, twenty-seven years his bloody war will last.*)

G.W. Bush
G. W. Bush = g.w. Bus(h) = M. a. Bus = Mabus?

Many would dispute Nostradamus labeling Napoleon Bonaparte one of his three Antichrists given the many positive legacies of a dictator who created the Code Napoleon, a foundation for modern European codes of law. Napoleon seemed more progressive and pro-Semitic than the popes. When he conquered the Papal States, he immediately freed the Jews from their Ghettos. As long as his sprawling European Empire lasted, Jews were given equal rights.

Each successive Antichrist becomes more outwardly violent and evil. It has also been proposed that a mediocre man given ultimate power can also elevate stupidity to a state of evil by abusing that power, leading a nation into ill-conceived military adventures draining its life blood and treasure.

Historians have not been kind when assessing the eight years of President Bush in office. Despite a number of CIA intelligence warnings he failed to prevent the terrorist attack on the US homeland, launched an ill-defined War on Terror, and soon got the US bogged down in a stalemate in Iraq lasting eight years and another dragging on for 12 years and counting in Afghanistan. He enacted the Patriot Act significantly undermining personal freedoms, launched a unilateral war on, and bloody occupation of, Iraq on a false premise that Saddam Hussein was hiding weapons of mass destruction. He punctuated insult with injury of his ending presidency with the Great Recession of 2008 and the bailout of the banking system that caused the Recession, with the money of its victims, the US taxpayers.

In 2008 I wrote:

> *President Bush may not be Mabus, the fallen catalyst for 27 years of war, but he may be remembered as catalyst for destabilizing and spiraling a world down into the arms of such an Antichrist thanks to the powers invested in idiocy that accelerated waste, pollution, ecological degradation, the unraveling of the Middle East and heightened the fever of global warming—all key factors foreseen by Nostradamus and many seers, ancient and modern, for triggering the derailment of civilization no later than the 2020s.*

Nostradamus and the Antichrist,
Chapter 8: g.w. Bush = m.a. Bus(h)

Usama bin Laden
Usama bin Laden = maaus b(in
Laden) = maabus = Mabus?

In the late summer of 2008, and many months before the presidential election was decided, the following Nostradamus verse inspired a prediction about Bush's successor, President Obama, and the fate of Usama bin Laden:

—w—

Sa main derniere par Alus fanguinaire
Ne fe pourra par la mer guarentir:
Entre deux fleuues craindre main militaire,
Le noir l'ireux le fera repentir.

His power finally through the bloody USA
He will be unable to protect himself by sea.
Between two rivers [Mesopotamia–
Iraq] **he will fear the military hand,**
The black king will make the
angry one repent of it.

6 Q33

A right interpretation depends on divining who is the subject of these vague third person personal and possessive pronouns. Play with it in French and the anagram *Alus sanguinaire* (Bloody Alus) becomes *L'USA sanguinaire* (the bloody USA). *Le noir* (the black) may be an anagram for *le roi n*(oir): "the black king." Earlier interpretations had a black robed Shia cleric of Iran or Iraq who makes the *angry one*, such as Saddam Hussein, repent; however, if this applies literally to an African American future president, then it might describe Barack Obama's Iraq policy in future action.

The Greek *Meso* (between) *potamia* (two rivers) is Iraq geographically defined as the land between the Tigris and Euphrates Rivers. This round of interpretation presumes President Bush the *angry one* made to repent his invasion of Iraq by Obama who pulls out combat troops in the first 16 months of his presidency. Another candidate for *angry one* is Usama bin Laden who *will repent* ordering al-Qaeda to infiltrate Iraq during the Bush administration. The *Black* president (*king*) will increase US forces in Afghanistan, killing or capturing Usama in a military incursion into Pakistan.

Nostradamus and the Antichrist,
Chapter 9: Obama the Mabus

—ᘏᘏ—

Obama was elected president and did achieve his promise of pulling out US combat troops in Iraq in 16 months. He then instigated a surge of US and NATO forces in Afghanistan, a huge surprise to anyone listening to his presidential campaign promises when I made this prediction. Usama bin Laden was killed by US Special Forces who landed by helicopter inside his Abbottabad, Pakistan, compound on the night of 2 May 2011 (local time). At the time of this writing, Usama and Saddam Hussein are tied fulfilling Nostradamus' clues. Here is the tally:

Both are dead candidates, the first and dubious milestone. Both violently annihilated: Saddam was hanged on 30 December 2006, Usama shot by US Navy seals on May Day (local Washington DC time) 2011.

(Score Saddam 1, Usama 1)

Both men's names can be found in the code name Mabus.

(Score Saddam 2, Usama 2)

The horrible undoing of people and animals has not been made clear in either dead candidate's case. On 13 May 2011, I wrote:

> *This, however, does not ignore the potential of either some terrible terrorist reprisal (in the case of Usama) or an unraveling of the Arab world because of a future breakup of Saddam's Iraq as causes for the unraveling of the world. Saddam had famously predicted*

> *before being hanged that without his strong hand and dictatorship, Kurd, Shia and Sunni Iraqi's would not be able to govern themselves and that sooner or later, Iraq would unravel. If the Middle East unravels, so does the oil industry that fuels human civilization.*

> *Is Osama or Saddam Nostradamus' Third Antichrist?*
> (Hogueprophecy.com,
> 13 May 2011)

They both score points if we take the view that a horrible undoing or unraveling of both people and animals is meant to date the time of their deaths tied to the present era of accelerating climate change:

(Saddam 3, Usama 3)

Now, if line three of 2 Q62 and part of line four are implying an alliance of 100 nations taking vengeance on a history-changing terrorist act, Usama's al-Qaeda 9/11 attacks did see President G. W. Bush collect 100 nations into his alliance to seek out and destroy Usama's terrorist network.

(Score: Saddam 3, Usama 4)

The last line of 2 Q62 returns to the theme of describing the times of the death of the Antichrist: a time of great climate disruption (thirst=drought), the crisis of potable water and famine looming for the overpopulated world, so, no score change.

(Score: Saddam 3, Usama 4)

Saddam scores with the reference to chemical weapons attacks in 8 Q77 killing over 5,000 Kurds in 1988 in Halabja, along with killing and crippling 100,000 Iranian soldiers during the Iran-Iraq War (1980-1988).

(Score: Saddam 4, Usama 4)

Now to 8 Q77's line 3. This one leans in favor of Usama. He and his al-Qaeda jihadists are each considered by a vast majority of Muslims around the world as *Al-muhartik* (heretic). Since 9/11 most of the leading al-Qaeda planners, the cream of his suicide operatives who committed the act and thousands of al-Qaeda foot soldiers, have been eliminated (*dead*), *exiled* from their countries of origin and made *captives* wasting away in a network of prisons far from home such as the US concentration camp at Guantanamo Bay, Cuba.

(Score: Saddam 4, Usama 5)

Line two of 8 Q77 says about the Third Antichrist, "27 years his bloody war will last."

Saddam fulfills this. The time he was made dictator, to the time he was hanged was 27 years of constant warfare for Iraq.

Score one for Saddam?

Not so fast!

Further in my May 2011 Hogueprophecy article (*Is Osama or Saddam Nostradamus' Third Antichrist?*), I reported:

Usama, back in 1984, established MAK (Maktab al-Khidamat) with Abdullah Azzam, an organization to raise funds and recruit a foreign legion of Arab mujahedeen fighters, mostly Saudi Arabs, to aid the Afghani mujahedeen's guerilla war against Soviet occupiers of Afghanistan. Although Usama had been funding and fighting alongside Afghans since he completed college in 1979, MAK put Usama on history's time map as a leader in a war—just the kind of prominence that a prophet from the sixteenth century would have recognized.

In 1984, Usama's bloody war began, first with the Soviets, and then four years later, MAK became the foundation for creating and fundraising and recruiting al-Qaeda. Usama's war shifted from Soviets and became a guerilla-terrorist war against Arab dictators, the Saudi King beholden to Western "Crusader" powers with a string terror bombings in the Middle East during the 1990s, as well as the first World Trade Center bombing in 1993.

Then came dramatic, large-scale swipes at US embassies in Kenya and Tanzania in 1998 killing hundreds and wounding thousands. Then the USS Cole bombing at port in Yemen in 2000 killing and wounding dozens of US Navy personnel...

Then came his bloody war's greatest terror act, the 9/11 toppling of the World Trade

Center twin towers and setting alight the US Pentagon with hijacked civilian airliners killing 3,000. This lead to US occupation of Afghanistan in a war spanning nearly a decade, killing over 50,000 civilians and combatants from all sides. The drone wars over Western Pakistan commenced, killing hundreds more. The war in Afghanistan spilled over into a conflict between Taliban Pakistani guerillas with the Pakistani Army adding thousands to the butcher bomber's bill.

Then Usama's blood war ended with his death by US Navy Seal bullets just a dozen days ago.

Usama's bloody war lasted from 1984 to 2011.

That is also 27 years!

Both Saddam and Usama win a point from me.

(Score: Saddam 5, Usama 6)

Mabus is soon annihilated and all these events transpire "when the comet will pass."

Usama died without a visible comet over the night skies of Abbottabad. Saddam did, Comet McNaught.

(Score tied)

Barack Obama
Obama = Ubama = maabu = Mabu(s) = Mabus

Barack Obama to his sympathizers and apologists may be as far removed from suspicion of being an antichrist as George Washington, Abraham Lincoln and John F. Kennedy, yet unlike these men his name is among the easiest to decode out of the code name for the Third Antichrist. First, follow the phonetics of his surname in Swahili: Obama is pronounced *ooh*-bama. Thus, word crunching *Ubama* gives us *maabu*. Drop the redundant "a" for the missing "s" and you have *Mabus*.

We have to consider all possibilities, even those that brand "antichrist" on charismatic men of powerful oratory who inspire lofty dreams and audacious hopes for change. Nostradamus' Second Antichrist, Adolf Hitler, once wrote in *Mein Kampf* that a man running for office must relate to the masses as if they were a woman. Appeal to emotion, not mind. Expansive dream weaving is good as long as you propagate a dream so generalized that anyone in the crowd can reflect their interpretation of the dream upon it. Keep the slogan simple. Keep the dream pure of price and consequence. Do not get trapped in the complexity of "how" you will bring change. How much it will cost each voter. Just promise change with all your heart. Believe it so deeply that what you persuade yourself to believe is transmitted and propagated to the people like *Baraka*—the Arabic word that is the basis for Obama's first name *Barack*—a term for spiritual grace and blessing descending from God.

The following was documented in July 2008, four months before Barack Obama was elected president:

Nostradamus, though a prophet on the periphery of mainstream eschatological thinking was nonetheless a Judeo-Christian seer. He used biblical metaphors for the Antichrist, such as Appalyon and Baal Hammon. Nostradamus as a part of the Judeo-Christian tradition need not spell out the background of what his predominantly Judeo-Christian readers, contemporary or future born, already read in the scriptures. They would know as he did, the Bible's signs of antichrist referenced in the Apocalypse of St. John.

To those who subscribe to beholding their antichrists in beastly Book-of-Revelation meter, the Antichrist will appear initially as an all powerful world leader and peacemaker. He rules a superpower nation or empire and wields complete military and economic authority to wage war or force his idea of peace and economy on anyone, anywhere in the world.

Tens of thousands of letters I receive from New-Age leaning to holy roller Judeo-Christian readers share the popular belief in a prophetic forbearance. A future antichrist begins his rule as an apparent bold and benevolent leader who has the guts to start cleaning up the world's rogue and terrorist harboring nations if no one else will. He does this through the power of his charismatic personality and mostly via diplomacy. He'll bring freedom and enlightenment to Iraq,

Iran, North Korea, etc. He will initially be successful and face little resistance at first from home or abroad. His enemies and critics will be divided and weak, his friends exultant and arrogant, while the majority is cautiously supportive, but generally in denial of his darker statements and documented plans.

Nostradamus and the Antichrist,
Chapter 9: Obama the Mabus

One radical theory I have already put forward considering G.W. Bush is that each Antichrist evokes a three-step decent into greater evil. The biblical tradition would either portray that evil becoming more subtle and seductive with the last advent of Antichrist; or, we overlook another kind of evil, more intimate, close to all of us, personified by the man who would be the Final Antichrist. That evil I call the *Antichrist Unconscious.*

It is a phenomenon of life being lived in a semiconscious state where we are programmed by society to think we live as awake and fully aware masters of our ideas and fate. It encompasses an unawareness of living life in the disguise of egoistic personalities, borrowing identities from our society and robotically playing these roles with open-eyes blind to a core reality. Most of our thoughts and feelings are borrowed and not an expression of our true nature and Existence-given spiritual intelligence. We thus live out our days and die mostly unaware of our inauthentically lived lives in a world where Stupidity and Mediocrity are the core evils aided and abetted by a civilization in name only, set up to stifle and delay progress in our humanitarian and spiritual development. That may be why history is a misery-go-round of repetitive tragedy, wars and misunderstanding. Prophecy can work well to foresee that kind of future, because until humanity matures and passes out of this bad habit of unconscious living, it will remain childishly predictable.

Framed in the light of this theory is Barack Obama. If he were the Antichrist Nostradamus actually intended, he represents the evil of good men who gain ultimate power without the consciousness, wisdom and talent such levels of leadership require. In short, it could be argued that like his predecessor George W. Bush, Obama, in the final reckoning of History, may be judged a disappointment—the evil inherent in a betrayal by a false promise of positive change—at a time when the world descending into planetary crisis has the greatest need for decisive leadership. All "feel-good" slogans aside, and all anticipations of Obama being some kind of messianic politician that could bring change the world believed in, he turns out instead to be a nice man embodying a well-intentioned mediocrity, disastrously wielding ultimate power, thus establishing that mediocrity as the ultimate evil.

The unintended consequences could be catastrophic. Obama has not effectively communicated or made America a leader taking the human civilization out of its fossil fuel addiction as promised in his presidential campaigns. Thus, the unraveling of the world of people and animals by global warming as foreseen in the Mabus quatrain has already begun on his watch!

This man was so potent in promising an anticipated greatness that the committee for the Nobel Peace Prize in September 2008 had secretly decided to award him the peace prize the following February. He had not been elected president or actually done anything to bring peace on Earth except make speeches about it!

Although his presidency did end the Iraqi occupation of his predecessor, President Obama has acquiesced playing a part in a vastly expanded global war on terrorists using robot planes and drones that seems only to have spread international terrorism. Rather than bring peace, he advocated war and NATO airstrikes in Syria (2013) after leading NATO airstrikes on Libya. The latter is now a failed state, the bones and ruins of which are fought over by warring militias and warlords. Libya is yet another unanticipated consequence of US military intervention not thought through with any realpolitik skill. Libya now is a tumor source for militant jihad spreading into the Western Sahara, Niger, Chad and Nigeria.

Indecision and procrastination played in Obama's enterprise to establish political, logistical and military aid for the burgeoning Syrian Resistance while it was secular and not overtaken later on by jihadist groups. When he at last did give aid, it went mostly to arm US enemies, al-Qaeda and ISIS in Syria. The latter used the weapons to conquer much of northwestern Iraq in the summer of 2014. ISIS would rout four US-armed and trained Iraqi Army divisions outside of Mosul adding to their arsenal billions of dollars worth of sophisticated US weaponry.

Obama seems unable to anticipate and prevent America's return to G.W. Bush's military quagmire that is Iraq, only the situation is far worse now. Iraq is breaking apart. This is fast becoming the dark-in-aspect land that Obama had serenely proclaimed at the end of US occupation was being left behind as "sovereign, stable and self reliant." It is instead an Islamo-fascist Lorelei, a siren of Islamic sectarian conflict calling him and Americans back into an uncertain future, waging war in yet another state ruined during his watch as president.

The most troubling of these failures as a global statesman, prophetically speaking, is Obama's inability to proactively stay ahead of and stave off a widening rift dividing Russia with the EU and US in a new Cold War. As we will examine next, the decisions he has made, and will make, may have already set in motion Nostradamus' countdown to a thermonuclear war between America and Russia.

In the dark and gathering storms of Nostradamian prophecy, one could envision that Obama was intended by the prophet to be Mabus. That is, if decisions he has made or did not make, bring on World War Three with Russia and he "soon dies" 30 minutes after Russian missiles reach Washington after launching, then, the "terrible destruction of people and animals" ensues from thousands of nuclear explosions wiping Russia and the US off the map. The dead and flaming cities deliver an outpouring of smoke that robs all warmth and light from the Sun as a reddened and icy hail covers the Earth. After that comes a great unraveling of people and animals. Famine nearly extinguishes the human race *and* the balance of nature on Earth is nearly destroyed.

The Great Brothers
The Northern Eagle Kings
Go to War

Vn iour feront demis les deux grands maiſtres,
Leur grand pouuoir ſe verra augmenté:
La terre neufue fera en ſes hauts eſtres,
Au ſanguinaire le nombre racompté

One day the two great lead-
ers will become friends,
Their great power will be seen to increase:

The new land [America] **will be
at the height of its power,
To the bloody one, the number is reported.**

2 Q89

The quatrain's indexing is the key unlocking
this prophecy dating the official end of the Cold
War in 1989. Century "2" stands for the second
month of 19[89]. In February 1989, Soviet forces
fighting and occupying Afghanistan for a decade
abandoned all hope of winning and departed.
By December 19[89] Soviet Premier Mikhail
Gorbachev and US President George Herbert
Walker Bush officially declared the Cold War
over. Soon after, the Soviet Union collapsed and
left the "new land" of America the supreme and
sole surviving superpower at the height of its
might. The *bloody one* is Gorbachev, identified by
his signature bloody birthmark on his balding
forehead. The *number reported* is the inventory
of US nuclear weapons slated for destruction as
part of the agreed amount under discussion of
an eventual 75-percent reduction of Soviet and
American nuclear weapons arsenals pledged
by Gorbachev and Bush Sr. when they signed
START (the Strategic Arms Reduction Treaty) in
July 1991.

There is danger hidden in the original spelling for "friends."

Nostradamus makes up a word, a Greco-French hybrid, *demis*. It could be code for the French *d'amis*—friends—yet it is applied here as a Greek tragic pun for being "halved" or "split." The friendship will not last; moreover, as America's power grows, so will what replaced the fallen Soviet Union, the Russian Federation and that will lead to future tensions.

& feront lors les Seigneurs deux en nombre d'Aquilon victorieux fur les orientaux, & fera en iceux faict fi grand bruict & tumulte bellique, que tout iceluy orient tremblera de l'effrayeur d'iceux freres non freres Aquilonaires.

And when shall the lords be two in number, victorious in the north against the [Middle] **Eastern ones, there shall be a great noise and warlike tumult that all the East shall quake for fear of those two *Aquilon* brothers of the North** [those represented by constellation of Aquila] **who are not yet brothers.**

EPISTLE

He is not describing Russia and America pitted in struggles in the Middle East during the Cold War because both here are identified by a classical metaphor, when, in ancient Roman times, the northern winds coming from the direction of the northern constellation of Aquila (the Eagle) marked the onset of winter. The great brothers are northern "Eagle" kings. The American leader identifies himself with the Bald Eagle. The President of the Russian Federation places on the presidential standard the golden double-headed eagle of the Czars. Moscow restored the double-eagle as its totem in 1992. Mark that time as activating these ominous prophecies for "our" times, starting from 1992 into the early Twenty-First Century.

The Middle *Eastern ones* in Iraq during the Persian Gulf War (1991) up through the US invasion and occupation of Iraq (2003-2011) experienced the warlike wrath and tumult of shock and awful US military might. The Chechen jihadist *eastern ones* felt a similar wrath and ruin descend upon them in two wars with Russia in 1994-1996 and 1999-2000. In the latter, the Chechen capital of Grozny was all but flattened by Russia's recovering military might.

After 1992 when President Bush stepped down from office, his successor, President Clinton, initiated NATO's steady encroachment eastward towards Russia, thus straining all future attempts at rapprochement and friendship between the great eagle brothers of the North.

> *Les deux vnis ne tiendront longuement,*
> *Et dans treze ans au Barbare Satrappe:*
> *Au deux coftez feront tel perdement,*
> *Qu'vn benira le Barque & fa cappe.*

The two united will not remain so for long,
And within thirteen years they give
in to a *Barbare* henchman.
There will be such a loss on both sides
That one will bless the barque and cape of pope.

5 Q78

Unlocking the meaning of *Barbare Satrappe* linguistically unseals the riddle's secret. A *Satrap* is a "henchman" or "proxy," a vassal servant of larger powers. Because the word is Persian in origin, it might imply modern Iran as the catalyst for a future war between the two brothers, having failed at brotherhood. Tensions have pushed Iran into Russia's sphere of influence ever since 1979 when the Islamic Revolution overthrew Iran's dictator and America's ally, Shah Reza Pahlavi, though Tehran is not a proxy or henchman to Moscow in the truest sense. We have to look at another clue to find the identity of the true henchman who triggers World War Three and that can be found in the anagram *Barbare*. It spells the French phrase *d'Arabe* ("of," or "from Arabs").

Simply follow Nostradamus' rules of anagram. The dropping of the redundant "r" and the turning of a redundant "b" to a "d" gives you the following word conversions:

Barbare = barba(r)*e =* (d)*arbae = darabe = d'Arabe*

Arab proxies of either the US or Russia some-how pull the brother eagle kings of the North into open conflict. Look then to Russia's ally, the Syrian dictator Bashar al-Assad and/or the American ally, the severe and dictatorial Islamic kingdom of Saudi Arabia as the cause.

A third and fearsome Arab Islamo-fascist "hench-man" and one-time tacit ally of the Americans can be uncovered by following Nostradamus' predictions concerning modern Iraq.

Let us fast "foreword" back to that future foreseen four-and-a half centuries ago, when Nostradamus predicted a modern "Crusader" army would occupy Mesopotamia (Iraq) and then foretold the outcome. Century 3, Quatrain 61 reads:

La grande bande & fecte crucigere,
Se dreffera en Mefopotamie:
Du proche fleuue compagnie legere,
Que telle loy tiendra pour ennemie.

The great host and sect of cross bear-ers [or: the Crusaders]**,**
Will be massed in Mesopotamia [Iraq]**:**
Of the nearby river [the Euphrates]
the fast company,
That such a law will hold for the enemy.

3 Q61

During the era of the Crusades, Western knights never invaded the region between the Tigris and Euphrates Rivers known as Mesopotamia, the ancient name of modern Iraq. The term *Crusaders* has since been used as a pejorative by various Islamo-fascist and jihadist organizations in their war against Western infidels from America or their EU allies invading and occupying Muslim lands in the Middle East. Eventually hundreds of thousands of these Crusaders amassed in Iraq after launching a blitzkrieg invasion of the *fast company* of American armored columns of Operation Iraqi Freedom racing out of Kuwait, driving swiftly up the west bank of the Euphrates before crossing over and seizing Baghdad.

Nostradamus picks the winner and it is not the Americans. The *law* of the enemy of these Crusaders holds. That means it "withstands," it "survives," it "wins" against whatever intrusions of Crusaders—came or perhaps would come again. The Islamic law of the Sharia in its darkest and most stark and fundamentalist interpretation "holds" in Iraq and that black future "enemy" just gets blacker as time goes on, according to Nostradamus.

Il entrera vilain, mefchant, infame,
Tyrannifant la Mefopotamie:
Tous amys faits d'adulterine d'ame,
Tertre horrible noir de phifonomie.

He will enter, wicked, unpleasant, infamous,
Tyrannizing over Mesopotamia [Iraq]
All friends made by the adulterous lady,
The land dreadful and black of aspect.

8 Q70

Nostradamus' quatrains become clearer as the times draw close to the events and details cloaked in their codes and riddles. The tyrant in question cannot be Saddam Hussein because he is not a foreigner entering Iraq such as the two Bush US presidents, father in 1991 and son in 2003, or some Middle Eastern invader.

He may be a one-time "Barbare"-Arab hench-man of America being that Nostradamus, a six-teenth-century royalist, accurately foresaw and hated the French Revolution, represented by the totem of Marianne. Americans had also adopted Marianne as their icon, the Statue of Liberty. It was a gift of the French reassembled on a pedes-tal that, ever since its dedication in 1886, towers over New York harbor.

Lady Liberty is America's "adulterous lady" in his prophecies. She has so far, in successive invasions and an occupation, choked Iraq's harsh desert landscape with the graves of over a mil-lion Iraqis since 1991. It could be argued that Lady Liberty wantonly ignores her constitutional constraints and debases the American dream of freedom when waging her aggressive wars and unilateral occupations for imperial profit. She covets Iraq's oil, damn the natives' death toll or what destabilizing social, economic and political outrages are left in her wake after she is satiated.

Verse 70 of Century 8 surrenders new potential insights from the future ever since ISIS exploded out of civil-war torn Syria in lightning fast fashion. Is not ISIS now entering Iraq, wickedly beheading and slaughtering those who do not convert to its ugly twisting of the Islamic holy law? Are they not black-cloaked hoods, waving their black flags as an unpleasant and infamous band of holy warriors, *tyrannizing over Iraq?*

We might refresh the interpretation of the previous 3 Q61 as one of Nostradamus' double entendres used to catch history repeating itself. Rather than solely describing a US invasion in 2003, the verse may also imply ISIS in 2014 as the "fast company" driving trucks and captured US armored personnel carriers and tanks, bedecked with black flags of jihad, sprinting down the river bank of the Tigris, seizing most of northwestern Iraq to create "IS" (the Islamic State). This IS is a new Caliphate (Islamic papacy, if you will) spreading its black flag and white-Arabic-lettered shadow over maps of northeastern Syria down into northwestern Iraq. The IS Caliphate's interpretation of Sharia Law is so vicious and cruel, even al-Qaeda has completely disowned them and units of al-Qaeda forces in the Free Syrian Army fight pitched battles with them. Moreover, the men of ISIS were once "friends" of the "adulterous" Lady Liberty.

In 2013, a picture was taken of US Senator of Arizona John McCain with leaders of ISIS, insinuating themselves as part of the rag-tag mix of jihadist and secular Sunni Muslim forces known as the Free Syrian Army fighting the Shia and Christian coalition forces of the al-Assad regime in the Syrian Civil War. ISIS fighters have already enjoyed clandestine CIA training and logistical support as well as shipments of US arms sent via a pipeline of US proxies, such as Saudi Arabia and Qatar. The *friends of the adulterous lady* appear to be ISIS officers and men, one day glad-handing Senator McCain in 2013, then the following year, entering Mesopotamia, "already" armed and supported by Lady-Liberty *Libertine* as a US ally in Syria.

Returning to 8 Q70 one could rework the verse so its says, "ISIS will enter, wicked, unpleasant, infamous, tyrannizing over Mesopotamia (Iraq). All friends made by the adulterous lady [Liberty]. Rendering Iraq a land dreadful and black of aspect. To those of the black flags of ISIS, to the Crusaders' black-hooded enemies, it is *their law* that shall *hold* victorious against the double-crossing cross bearers.

That is, unless history repeats for ISIS in the future what it did to al-Qaeda when it tried occupying Iraq in the past.

Sa main derniere par Alus fanguinaire
Ne fe pourra par la mer guarentir:
Entre deux fleuues craindre main militaire,
Le noir l'ireux le fera repentir.

His power finally through bloody Alus,
He will be unable to protect himself by sea.
Between two rivers he will fear
the military hand,
The black one [black king?] **will**
make the angry one repent of it.

6 Q33

Main in Old French is used figuratively signifying *power*, symbolized as the king's chain-mailed weapon hand. It looks clearer now that the possessor of this "hand" of power is the leader of ISIS and his power has been enabled by "bloody Alus." This "Alus" is an anagram returning us to the "Adulterous Lady" America theme, because the French spelling of the acronym for the United States is Alus = *l'USA* (the USA). The American military hand struck fear in Saddam Hussein during the Persian Gulf War (1991) and similarly eradicated the black-clad warriors of the guerilla force known as "al-Qaeda in Mesopotamia" during the last sectarian civil war in Iraq (2006-2008). Likewise, the leader of ISIS cannot protect himself from US Navy jets and missiles launched from American ships stationed in the Persian Gulf who can fire with impunity, safe from counterattacks.

The emergence of ISIS as a real player in this prophecy only muddies up the nebulous use of syntax by Nostradamus in the final two lines. Just which "he" fears the "military hand" of whom?

Is "his hand" mentioned in line one linked to the leader in line two representing successive Iraqi Shi'ite prime ministers kept in power by US manipulation in Baghdad? Perhaps they fear the military "power" of ISIS as it rampages towards Baghdad between the two rivers (*Meso* [between] *potamia* [rivers], i.e. modern Iraq)?

On the other hand, is "he" the leader of ISIS fearing the military *hand* grasping the joystick of a computer console electronically guiding by satellite link a US drone on the other side of the Earth? It flies in Iraqi skies on the hunt for assassinating ISIS leaders by drone-fired missiles in a "decapitation" mission. Is it the living hand of US pilots directing fighter bombers in airstrikes sending fire down on ISIS motorized columns advancing on the road to Baghdad between the bottleneck of the Tigris and Euphrates Rivers?

Who then is *Le noir*, the "black one"?

Is it the black-turbaned and robed leader of ISIS, the Islamic State's Caliph Ibrahim, AKA Abu Bakr al-Baghdadi? Or, is this a repetition of Nostradamus' anagram: *Noir*, "black" representing *roi* N(egro) illustrating he is an African American "king", or "President" Barack Obama? In this slant, the final line could predict the sudden annihilation of a fifth major candidate for Nostradamus' final Antichrist: "The Black King Obama will make the Angry one, Caliph Ibrahim (M)abu(S) Bakr, "repent of it."

At the time of this writing, ISIS and its leader would seem best positioned to be the "Barbare" henchman, especially if he "soon dies" or is "martyred" (annihilated) by the US military hand reaching out from the sea. Before this happens he possibly commits an outrage so dastardly, that it drags the Great Brothers into a nuclear conflict in 13 years, or even sooner:

> *La regne à deux laiffé bien peu tiendront,*
> *Trois ans fept mois paffés feront la guerre,*
> *Les deux veftales contre rebelleront,*
> *Victor puis nay en Armorinque terre.*

The rule left to two [America and Russia?]
They will hold it for a very short time.
Three years and seven months having passed,
they will go to war.
Their two vassals [Barbare henchmen?] **rebel against them.**
The victor is born on American soil.

4 Q95

As with many of Nostradamus' chillingly accurate countdowns of periods of time in history, he coyly gives little clue for when one should start the countdown. Let us say we start counting from the beginning of a new cold war over the Crimea and Ukrainian crisis of 2014 and the invasion of ISIS occupying large tracts of Iraq. That could mean the short countdown could bring on the thermonuclear war described by Nostradamus in the following and terrifying prophecies as soon as the first year in office of the next US president, elected in 2016.

This count would shine a completely new and apocalyptic light on the Mabus and Third Antichrist verses:

[M]**Abu**[s al-Baghdadi] **will
soon die, then will come,
A horrible undoing of people
and animals…** (2 Q62)
**The Third Antichrist very soon annihilated…
The heretics** [are] **dead, captives exiled.
Blood-soaked human bodies,
and a reddened, icy hail [nuclear fallout from a Nuclear Winter?]
covering the earth.** (8 Q77)

There is a collective vision coming from those prophets down through history who, along with Nostradamus, have clearly dated and described in detail our future world wars. Nearly all of them foresee not two but THREE world wars, the last of which is engaged after the resumption of a Cold

War between Russia and America in which the Middle East plays the match lighting the nuclear fires of the following:

Sera laiffé le feu vif, mort caché,
Dedans les globes horrible efpouuentable,
De nuict à claffe cité en poudre lafché,
La cité à feu, l'ennemy fauorable.

There will be let loose liv-
ing fire and hidden death.
Horror inside dreadful globes.
By night the city will be reduced
to dust by the fleet.
The city on fire, helpful to the enemy.

5 Q8

Soleil levant vn grand feu l'on verra,
Bruit & clarté vers Aquilon tendants:
Dedans le rond mort & cris l'on orra,
Par glaiue, feu, faim, mort las attendants.

At sunrise one will see a great fire.
Noise and light extending towards
[*Aquilon*-Eagle kings of] **the North.**
Within the earth death and cries are heard.
Death awaiting them through weap-
ons, fire and famine.

2 Q91

In *A New Cold War: The Prophecies of Nostradamus, Stormberger and Edgar Cayce,* I interpreted these verses as follows:

> *The living fire of the Sun, the human-invented Sun-fire of thermonuclear weapons, detonate and leave behind in the smoking darkness a hidden death of radiation fallout to sicken and kill all those left un-skeletonized by atomic fire. Nostradamus has looked deep into our future and seen underneath the casing of atomic weapons the dreadful spherical-shaped atomic-bomb triggering device of a fusion warhead. These* dreadful globes *can turn a city into glowing, radioactive dust.*
>
> *Nostradamus furthermore seems to be aware of nuclear war targeting protocols. The first missiles fired by Russia and America from their silos, submarines, or strategic bombers, fall like Nostradamus' running comet striking the southernmost targets then spreading their mini-Sun fireballs in a carpet-bombing pattern advancing northwards. Nostradamus hears our lament and death rattle while cloistered in the darkness of bomb shelters. Death waits to claim billions of us first through atomic weapons and radioactive firestorms destroying our cities, then follows the famine.*

*It is famine, more than fallout or blast
effects that will kill the vast majority of us
in a thermonuclear war. When thousands
of ports and cities go up in nuclear flame
and smoke, not only are the means to grow
food and transport foodstuffs destroyed but
the dust and smoke sent into the stratosphere
by nuclear detonations could block out the
Sun's rays from 18 months to two years in a
"Nuclear Winter." Crops feeding humanity
will starve of sunlight and warmth. Most of
you will starve and wither away like them.*

It is most important to be reminded after encountering such horrific visions, that Nostradamus
believed in free will and often provided alternative futures that individuals and collective nations
alike could choose. Even Armageddon can be
avoided, but it will take a new religious revolution in consciousness sparked by a future world
teacher who is the antidote to the Antichrist.

Has he already come?

Have we missed the signs?

chapter three

The Man From The East

Tant attendu ne reuiendra iamais,
Dedans l'Europe, en Afie apparoiftra:
Vn de la ligue yflu du grand Hermes,
Et fur tous Roys des orients croiftra.

Long awaited he will never return.
He will appear in Asia [and
be] at home in Europe:
One who is issued from great Hermes,
And over all the Kings of the
East will he grow.

10 Q75

Nostradamus has made it clear that the next great spiritual master is coming from the East. He had to cloak his revelation so as not to be burned as a heretic. But if one can perceive the subtle message hidden between the lines of dozens of prophecies, it is clear that he is warning us not to look for the second coming of some gentile made-over blond and blue-eyed Hollywood

Jesus, nor should we expect some dark-haired and kosher man from Galilee named Yeshua.

The *Long awaited* projection of Jesus Christ we have created *will never return.*

The new world teacher will be from India or the Far East. He will issue from the non-dualistic teachings of Hermes. The Hermetic message is very close to the Eastern Tantric path, which teaches, "As above, so below; all is divine." In the Hermetic and Tantric paths, there is no Hell to fear or Heaven to pine for. These are childish illusions. No God exists outside of you. Without your awakened eyes and heart, God cannot perceive or love his universe. Without your understanding rising free of judgments and conditioning, there is no transcendental state of God. Without your enlightenment, God is as fast asleep as you are. In short, the Hermetic and Tantra visions propose that your existence is either a paradise or a hell of your own making, and no savior will be coming to carry your burdens. The Aquarian Age is about impersonal, or better, *transpersonal*, messianic phenomena. No sheep, no shepherds, no bleeding messiahs. The masters of the future may point the way, but it is your life to live and your universe to explore and celebrate.

Nostradamus describes this world teacher living in the manner of Hermes, who was also worshipped as a God of Thieves. This new "Jesus" is a very different "thief in the night" than the one expected by mainstream religions. He is from India, perhaps. This man represents a new understanding of *Harideva*: a Hindu metaphor for the divine as a stealer of hearts.

Whether the many gurus and god men bringing the spiritual values of the East to the Western world for over a century-and-counting are charlatans or true shamans of a new religiousness is still unknown. What is certain is that the seeds of a century of Eastern teachers have been planted in Western hearts and minds. We await their full flowering in the twenty-first century.

The quatrain's indexing may give us a hint of a key year for the advent to the West of Nostradamus' Man from the East: "Q75" = 1975, the year Madame Blavatsky, the Russian seeress and founder of Theosophy, predicted the appearance of "a messenger to come to the West in 1975."

Celuy qu'aura la charge de deftruire
Temples, & fectes, changez par fantafie:
Plus aux rochiers qu'aux viuans viendra nuire,
Par langue ornee d'oreilles reffafie.

A man who will be charged with destroying
Temples and sects altered by fantasy:
He will harm the rocks rather than the living,
Ears filled with ornate speeches.

1 Q96

The idea that traditional religions are a fantasy or a shadow of their original living teaching is a recurring theme for Nostradamus. The man mentioned here must be a pioneering mystic who will strike out against old rocklike dogmas, earning the unified wrath of the world's organized religions. We will know him as an eloquent and compelling speaker. The Indian mystic Osho was put in chains in America in 1985. Unification Church leader Sun Myung Moon was vilified. He was first imprisoned by the North Koreans and later served a term in prison in America. Bahá'í mystic 'Abdu'l-Bahá and his father before him (Bahá'u'llah) spent much of their lives in exile or in prison for their beliefs and teachings.

The year 1996 marks the beginning of a century-long decline of orthodox religions if the quatrain's indexing is a hidden date. By the year, 2096 they will have completely faded away or changed beyond recognition.

Nostradamus' Eight Clues
To the Founder of the coming Spiritual Revolution

A number of Nostradamus' prophecies seem to chronicle the lives and wisdom seed-planting actions of spiritual teachers and their movements from no later than the second half of the twentieth century. The pattern of these prophecies indicates the unique historical phenomenon we call the Human Potential or New Age movement.

Within this movement are many groups (both fraudulent and genuine) that experiment with alternative lifestyles, philosophies, and religions, often Eastern in origin, and practice new psychological and physical therapies. These groups, although not always in agreement over details, are mostly concerned with discovering new paths to world peace and ecological balance. All strive to awaken humankind to its potential for higher consciousness.

These prophecies can be gathered into eight specific categories. They are the prophet's eight clues to the character of this coming new *religiousness*, its non-dogmatic and individualistic teachings, and to the identification of its visionaries.

The eight clues and their corresponding quatrains are:

Clue 1. A Man from the East will be at Home in the West. A great spiritual catalyst from Asia finds his teachings welcomed in the West, primarily in Europe and America. Nostradamus maps out his flight to Europe, crossing the Apennine Mountains of Italy to first see France.

Dedans l'Europe, en Afie apparoiftra… (10 Q75)

L'Oriental fortira de fon fiege, paffer
les monts Apennins voir la Gaule:
Tranfpercera le ciel… (2 Q29)

He will appear in Asia [and be] **at
home in Europe...** (10 Q75)

**The man from the East will come out of his
seat, passing across the Apennines to see
France. He will fly through the sky...** (2 Q29)

Clue 2. The *Rod* **of Hermes** (after the cadu-
ceus wand of Hermes) indicates the teaching is
non-dualistic.

*Tranfpercera le ciel, les eaux & neige, et vn
chafcun frappera de fa gaule.* (2 Q29)

*Du pont Euxine, & la grand Tartarie,
vn Roy fera qui viendra voir la Gaule:
tranfpercera Alane & l'Armenie, et dans
Bifance lairra fanglante Gaule.* (5 Q54)

*...Dedans l'Europe, en Afie apparoiftra: Vn de
la ligue yflu du grand Hermes...* (10 Q75)

**...He will fly through the sky, the rains and the
snows and strike everyone with his rod.** (2 Q29)

**From the Black Sea, and great Tartary. There
will be a king who will come to see France:**
[He] **will penetrate through Russia and
Armenia, and into Byzantium** [Istanbul]**,
he will leave his bloody rod.** (5 Q54)

**...He will appear in Asia, at home in Europe.
One who is issued from great Hermes...**
(10 Q75)

Clue 3. Outlawed Teacher. The status quo religions will try to prevent this teacher from traveling freely around the world. This rebel mystic will harm the "rocks" of religious dogma rather than the existential religious nature of the living who are metaphorically imprisoned inside of them. The eloquence of this traveler will crack open the dogma rock and awaken the seed of religiousness in the listener.

*Celuy qu'aura la charge de deftruire temples, &
fectes, changez par fantafie: plus aux rochiers qu'aux
viuans viendra nuire, par langue ornee d'oreilles
reffafie.* (1 Q96)

**A man will be charged with destroying the temples
and religions altered by fantasy. He will harm the
rocks rather than the living. Ears filled with
ornate speeches.** (1 Q96)

Clue 4. Mystic Rose. The *rose* or *red* colors, along with all the red shades of sunset, symbolize the teachings from the East and are applied to the colors worn by disciples of the Eastern teachers. The "middle" way, a Buddhist teaching, is also implied. It gains greater popularity in the West at a time when the plague of war increases, as during our own times. Know this mystic is among us when silence is his message—his truth. Know also, that he will come late, as truth always does to a world that nourishes the egoist in all of us. The majority of us will recognize him after he is long dead. The "red ones" gathering around him are red-cloaked disciples that will live in controversy and persecution from the mainstream world. Know that the Man from the East, and his message of silence and peace, comes before the advent of the Third Antichrist (prior to the passing of the Comet Hale-Bopp in 1996-1997 or Comet McNaught in 2006-2007).

Sur le milieu du grand monde la roſe, pour nouueaux faicts ſang public eſpandu: a dire vray on aura bouche cloſe, lors au beſoing viendra tard l'attendu.
(5 Q96)

Contre les rouges ſectes ſe banderont, feu, eau, fer, corde par paix ſe minera, au point mourir, ceux qui machineront, fors vn que monde ſur tout ruynera.
(9 Q51)

Upon the middle of the great world—the rose. For new deeds public blood shed. To speak the truth they will have closed mouths. Then at the time of need the awaited one will come late.
(5 Q96)

**Against the red sects, religions will conspire.
Fire, water, steel, the [ac]cord through peace
to weaken. On the point of dying, those who will
contrive, except one who above all the world
will ruin.** (9 Q51)

Clue 5. Mars and Flame. The new religious rebellion symbolized by a *red*-as-revolution *flame* is poised to burn down the dogmas of the past. Many prophets foresee a purification of humanity *by fire*. It is for us to choose whether this fire is one of global warming, a third world war of international terrorism, or a fire of new religious self-awareness and consciousness. It will be a time when mainstream religions are racked with scandals and corruption. The people of that day will ask why they slavishly adopted into their lives what appear ever more clearly to be outmoded and even fossilized religious traditions.

> *...Et eftant proche d'vne autre defolation, par lors qu'elle fera à fa plus haute & fublime dignité... à ce que naiftra d'vn rameau de la fterille, de long temps, qui deliurera le peuple vniuers de celle feruitude benigne & volontaire foy remettant à la protection de Mars... de telle fecte fera fon eftendue par l'vniuers...*(Epistle to Henry II)

...At the eve of another desolation when the perverted church is atop her most high and sublime dignity... there will proceed one born

**from a branch long barren, who will deliver
the people of the world from a meek and
voluntary slavery and place them under the
protection of Mars. ...The flame of a sect shall
spread the world over...** (Epistle to Henry II)

Clue 6. Diana *Dhyana*, The *Moon* and Meditation.
The Science of Self-Observation is the fundamental tenet of the next global religion. The
Moon applies either to the feminine and intuitive
aspects of the new religion or to the name of one
or more of the spiritual catalysts.

*Vous verrez toft & tard faire grand change, horreurs
extremes & vindications: que fi la lune conduicte par
fon ange, le Ciel s'approche des inclinations.* (1 Q56)

*Le penultiefme du furnom du prophete, prendra
Diane pour fon iour & repos...* (2 Q28)

*Le tant d'argent de Diane & Mercur, les fimulacres
au lac feront trouuez: le figulier cherchant argille
neufue, luy & les fiens d'or feront abbreuez.*
(9 Q12)

*La Lune au plain de nuict fur le haut mont, le
nouueau fophe d'vn feul cerueau l'a veu: par fes
difciples eftre immortel femond, yeux au midy, en
feins mains, corps au feu.* (4 Q31)

Sooner and later you will see great changes, extreme horrors and vengeances. For the Moon is led by its angel. The heavens approach the Balance. [Astrological dating—Pluto transit of Libra 1972-1984] (1 Q56)

Second to the last of the prophet's name will take Diana's day (the Moon's day) as his day of silent rest... (2 Q28)

The great amount of silver of Diana [Moon] **and Mercury** [Hermes]. *The images will be seen in the lake* [a metaphor for the still mind in meditation]. **The sculptor looking for new clay. He and his followers will be soaked in gold** [a Hermetic reference to the attainment of enlightenment]. (9 Q12)

The Moon in the middle of the night... The young sage alone with his mind has seen it. His disciples invite him to become immortal...His body in the fire. (4 Q31)

Clue 7. The Infuriating Traveler. The more controversial the globetrotting spiritual catalyst is, the more likely he is a visionary Nostradamus intended. No spiritual teacher in history has been accepted by the mainstream religions while they are alive. They are called mind-controllers and cultists today just as Buddha, Muhammad and Jesus Christ were called when they walked the Earth.

Prendra Diane pour ſon iour & repos: loing vaguera par frenetique teſte, et deliurant vn grand peuple d'impos. (2 Q28)

...[He] **will take Diana's day as his day of silent rest. He will travel far and wide in his drive to infuriate, delivering a great people from subjection.** (2 Q28)

Clue 8. Strange Birds crying *"Now!"* The strange *birds* are the spiritual *teacher* and his disciples calling upon humanity to wake up *now* before it is too late.

...en apres l'antechriſt fera le prince infernal, encores par la derniere foy... tous les Royaumes de la Chreſtienté, & auſſi des infideles, par l'eſpace de vingt cinq ans, & feront plus grieues guerres & batailles, & feront villes, citez, chaſteaux, & tous autres edifices bruflez, defolez...& tant de maux ſe commettront par le moyen de Satan, prince infernal, que preſque le monde vniuerſel ſe trouuera defaict & defolé: & auant iceux aduenements, aucuns oyſeaux infolites crieront par l'air. Huy, huy, & feront apres quelque temps eſuanouys. (Epistle to Henry II)

...The Antichrist returns for the last time...All the Christian and infidel nations will tremble...

for the space of twenty-five years. Wars and battles will be more grievous than ever. Towns, cities, citadels and all other structures will be destroyed...So many evils by Satan's prince will be committed that almost the entire world will find itself undone and desolated. Before these events many rare birds will cry in the air. 'Now!' 'Now!' and sometime later will vanish.

(Epistle to Henry II)

The Eleven Candidates For the Man from the East

In this section we will consider eleven personalities in the light of the prophet's Eight Clues who plant the seed for a spiritual rebellion in the latter half of the twentieth century, which will eventually bloom as a response to the travails about to overtake us in the twenty-first century. Nostradamus narrows the choices of candidates to those either coming from the East or Westerners drawing most of their inspiration from Eastern, non-dualistic teachings. Their advent window is limited to the second-half of the twentieth century. A third requirement is that the teacher will be a rebel, even in the eyes of his own Eastern religious roots. More than this, we will know he is the one foreseen by Nostradamus if he upsets all sides on the religious debate while alive, yet leaves behind a vibrant and spreading movement of disciples.

Swami Paramahansa Yogananda
(1893-1952)
Bengali Indian Mystic, Founder of the Self-Realization Fellowship

He introduced Kriya Yoga to the West and taught that the mind and heart could be raised from a limited moral consciousness into union (yoga) with the consciousness of God. Yogananda and his disciples sometimes wore orange robes in the Eastern tradition of the seeker (see Clue 5). One can apply to Yogananda Nostradamus' references to a man from the East, colors of flame, teachings flowering in the West, intensive travel. Yogananda's desire to synthesize the beliefs of the established religions of the world make him unlikely to be the one against whom *religions will unite* (see Clue 4). The new millennium has seen Yogananda and his followers rapidly distance themselves from any action or religious concept that one could deem as opposed by established religion and his movement has blended with all the ever more religiously correct movements of what is called the Mind-Body-Spirit, or New Age mainstream.

Meher Baba
(1894-1969)
Indian Sufi Mystic

Meher Baba, a Parsi, born in Pune, India, was a master of the devotional path of Sufism. He was

opposed to religious hierarchy, ritual, and cere-
mony, and his motto was, "Don't worry, be happy."
His followers set up "Baba Lover" centers all over
the world and, in America alone, Baba's teaching attracted an estimated 6,000 disciples. He was
indeed a rebel, but a peaceful one: his teachings
were neither inflammatory nor designed to anger
the established religions—he was no infuriating
traveler (see Clue 7). Although his philosophy
did include the concept of living in the *Now*
(Clue 8), it contains no bird symbolism, no Moon
aspect—either symbolic or actual—(see Clue 6),
and no mention of either the color red (see Clue
4), or of flames (see Clue 5). His movement has
steadily declined since his passing in 1969.

Swami Prabhupada
(1896-1978)
Founder of the Hare Krishna Movement

This Indian mystic came to the West during
the late 1960s to spread the message of Krishna
Consciousness initially among the flower children and hippie movements of that day, but later
found a wider mainstream audience. In the East,
the many shades of red in a flame are one of the
symbols of consciousness. Prabhupada's singing
and dancing Western followers wear the orange
robes of ancient Krishna devotees.

Prabhupada's teachings, although new
for people in the West, are based on ancient

Hindu-Vedic scriptures, and he encouraged his Western disciples to adopt the lifestyles prescribed by those traditional texts. Although the orange-robed Hare Krishnas have angered some and mostly puzzled many Westerners, it cannot be said that mainstream society views their existence as a dangerous threat to organized religious thinking. The movement has not significantly grown in size since the mid-1980s and seems to have passed its peak.

L. Ron Hubbard
(1916-1986)
Author of Dianetics™,
Founder of the Church of Scientology

Scientology aims to help people recover spiritual health after suffering psychic and mental traumas, guiding them on the path towards reestablishing a "clear" mental and spiritual state. The creator of Scientology, and his "new" religion itself, have encountered opposition around the world and fought many legal and political battles. It is considered dangerous by many established religions. The Scientology movement did, however, enter the twenty-first century with a continued, yet slow, increase of adherents (and controversy) making it a new religion worth watching which by 2002 had, by the Church's own count five million followers.

Hubbard drew most of his fundamental ideas for Scientology from Hinayana Buddhism and mainstream psychology. Thus his "new" religion is a repackaging of a traditional Eastern and Buddhist dogma; or, *from the East* (see Clue 1)— even though he is not from the East himself. One of its symbols is a flaming volcano (see Clue 5). Hubbard was not born under *Mars* (see Clue 5), has no Moon connection (see Clue 8), and does not follow a Hermetic tradition (see Clue 2). The Church by 2014 has an estimated 3.5 million adherents (by its own reckoning). This means it has lost 2.5 million in the last dozen years and may be either entering either a plateau period or a gradual decline.

'Abdu'L-Baha
(1844-1921)
Leader of the Bahá'í faith

The eldest son and successor of Bahá'u'lláh, assumed full authority for the Bahá'í movement upon his father's passing. He interpreted teachings that pave the way for a synthesis of all religions in a spiritual global village. Throughout much of his adult life, he spread the faith from Mt. Carmel in Palestine. Like his father, he had a prodigious correspondence with believers and inquirers around the globe, and endured long years of prison life. He made extensive tours to Europe and America and was a prophetic advocate for a League of Nations. The Bahá'í movement and its founding masters are Eastern (Iranian). They initially provoked controversy in the West; however, their promotion of interfaith openness soon became mainstream in the twentieth century and thus the movement has not been universally rejected as a cult by orthodox faiths, except by fundamentalist Islam. The new century sees millions of Bahá'í's continue spreading their religion the world over, and although their message of peaceful rebellion through diplomacy has great merit, the movement does not conform to all of Nostradamus' eight clues.

G.I. Gurdjieff
(1866-1949)
Master of The Fourth Way

Gurdjieff was born in Alexandropol in Russian Armenia. For some 20 years, his obsession to understand life's strange and mysterious phenomena drove him to travel throughout the remotest regions of Tibet, Central Asia, and the Middle East. Leaving Russia after the Bolshevik takeover, he established a communal spiritual campus outside of Paris in 1922, and later set up a Gurdjieff school in America. His teachings are a revolutionary synthesis of Eastern Christian, Sufi, Central Asian and South Asian techniques of meditation and awareness training which he called "The Fourth Way"—the other orthodox paths being the way of the yogi, the devotee, and the sadhu. In 1924 he disbanded the Mystery School and devoted himself to recording his teachings in three volumes: *Beelzebub's Tales to his Grandson, Meetings with Remarkable Men,* and finally *Life is real only then when "I am."* From 1933 onwards, he lived almost exclusively in Paris. His written teachings are a perennial fixture in the Mind-Body-Spirit genre. The new millennium sees Gurdjieff study and dancing groups continue to thrive all over the world. The generally exclusive quality of his mystery schools, notwithstanding their great merit, do not indicate any significant worldwide spread of his band of "religiousness" to the mainstream. Nor do the orthodox religions unanimously consider his teachings a particular threat.

Swami Satya Sai Baba
(1925-2011)
Siddhi Yogi

This man proclaimed himself the reincarnation of the Moslem mystic Sai Baba (1856-1916). He was a noted miracle worker, with millions of disciples in India and a more modest following in the West. In the Hindu tradition of sannyas, (seeker and follower) he wore orange robes and never traveled to the West. His teachings are primarily Hindu-fundamentalist mainstream. There was no

Hermetic aspect to his work (see Clue 2). Of the eleven candidates we are considering, Satya Sai Baba has one of the largest followings, but his movement is confined mainly to India. Though his teachings do not constitute any threat to international authorities, an assassination attempt was made on his life in June 1993 by former disciples with connections to extreme Hindu fundamentalist groups. Since the mid-1980s, no significant spread of interest has taken place, and there are signs that outside India his movement is gradually losing momentum.

Sun Myung Moon
(1920-2012)
Founder of Unification Church

Sun Myung Moon's Church has come into conflict with the authorities on numerous occasions and, as a result, Moon had spent time in jail. With a linguistic stretch, his last name phonetically at least coincides with Nostradamus' prediction that the leader will be associated with the Moon, *la lune* (see Clue 6)—that is, if Nostradamus was playing around with French words hiding English meanings. Moon had antagonized many people with his claim that he was the Christ of the second coming prophecies of the Christian Bible. Adherence to his Church caused much grief and anger, with disciples splitting ties with families. Though the press made much of this, the label, "family breaker" could be pinned on any authentic spiritual mystic who bids a devotee drop what he or she is doing, sever worldly ties and come follow. Christ often cited quotes from the Prophet Micah warning that he came as a home breaker setting sons against fathers, daughters against mothers, and so on. Moon had traveled extensively and his symbol was a red rising Sun in the east. He was an arch anti-communist (*delivering a great people from subjection* [see Clue 5]).

After Moon was released from jail in 1986, his ministry had gone significantly mainstream allying itself closely with the right-wing Christian fundamentalist movement in the American Republican Party. Mainstream evangelist leaders such as Jerry Falwell embraced him. Evidence supports the contention that Moon's Unification Church had been a major financial supporter of former president Reagan and George Bush, Sr. Though Moon resembles more clues than any other teacher examined thus far, he lived out his days turning, it seems, into a politically correct religious insider rather than a spiritual rebel. No connections with Hermes (Clue 2) are evident. By claiming himself to be the messianic successor to the founder of one of the major orthodox religions does not make him the foretold catalyst of a new religion. The Man from the East will not come to renew the "rocks" of an old dogma. Moon did not come to destroy and replace them altogether.

Adi Da Samraj
(1939-2008)
American mystic

Adi Da Samraj (previously known as Bubba and Da Free John) was an unpredictable American mystic who called himself a Master of the Heart. He taught self-transcendence or union with God, otherwise known as Divine Consciousness. This is a Hermetic teaching that works through self-observation of each moment—"now" (see Clue 8). Adi Da had suffered considerable persecution from organized religions and governments.

Adi Da is not from the East (see Clue 1), although he was a disciple of masters in India and his teachings have Eastern origins. He did, however, make the controversial claim to be the reincarnation of the nineteenth-century Indian swami, Vivekananda (1863-1902), who could be called one of the first mystical trailblazers "from the East" bringing Eastern teachings to Europe and America. Corporeal conundrums aside, Adi Da had traveled extensively and lived in India as a disciple before his self-realization. His teachings are unquestionably related to the Eastern *flame* (see Clue 4) and the symbolic Martian *red* (see Epistle quote—Clue 5). No significant relationship exists to *birds*: the Free Diast movement uses as its symbol the Dawn Horse, a prehistoric variant of Kalki, the White Horse of Hindu prophetic tradition that signifies Adi Da's claim to be the tenth and final Avatar (Messiah) of the Hindu prophetic tradition.

The mid-1990s had seen another transformation of Adi Da's name and teaching style; yet, the scope of his movement was limited compared with the burgeoning increase in the followings of Maharishi Mahesh Yogi or Osho.

Swami Maharishi Mahesh Yogi
(1911-2008)
Founder of the Transcendental Meditation Movement (TM)

A former physicist, born in northern India, this leader founded the highly successful TM Movement, now practiced by millions in the West as a technique for personal stress reduction and the attainment of inner tranquility. He had also traveled widely and provoked considerable controversy, especially during the 1960s when he became the "guru" of the Beatles. TM has taproots in the ancient Hindu Vedic Scriptures and seems now to have been largely accepted by orthodox religions as representative of the New Age movements. It was taught in Western colleges until 1977.

The Maharishi and the TM movement have survived to see the new millennium; however, the now late Maharishi's generally diplomatic integration with the religious mainstream preclude him from fulfilling Nostradamus' forecast of the new world teacher from the East being one who will shake down the dogmas of fossilized religious thought.

Osho
(Formerly known as Bhagwan Shree Rajneesh)
1931-1990
Indian philosopher

A former philosophy professor from India, this man and his following was front-page news all over the world during the 1980s. His red-clad followers, called Neo-Sannyasins, have taken part in his experimental communes in India, Europe and in the US. Political, local and religious controversy surrounds him and his memory even well into the new millennium. Osho's spontaneous daily discourses on love and meditation embraced a wide range of subjects, from sex to superconsciousness. His merciless, humor-filled insights into man's unconscious and conditioned behavior, and his uncompromising critical view of political and religious institutions as a mafia of the soul, have earned him unanimous rejection by all mainstream religions. In the mid-1980s, Osho was arrested, jailed and then deported from the United States. After his departure, his attempt to go on a world religious tour met with strong political and theological opposition and he was expelled from, or denied entry to, 21 countries in the space of only five short months.

His followers allege that pressure from the Christian-fundamentalist-controlled Reagan government used threats to persuade other governments to keep their borders closed to the mystic. An example of this is detailed in investigative reporter Max Brecher's book *A Passage to America.* Osho was one step away from being granted permanent residency in Uruguay when, according to Brecher's highly-placed sources, the Uruguayan president Sanguinetti received a phone call from the American Ambassador Malcolm Wilkey, who said, "You are a free country. You can do what you want. But you owe the United States six billion dollars. And this is the year for renegotiating a new loan. If you do not make your payments on time, we will raise the interest rates."

Sanguinetti discovered and relayed to Osho's entourage, residing in Punta del Este, that the thinly veiled threat hinged on Uruguay granting Osho permanent residency. The Uruguayan government decided not to grant permanent residency to the mystic and he was "invited to leave." Not long afterwards Sanguinetti was invited to the Reagan White House, where it was announced that Uruguay's loan would be, after all, extended, and that his country would be the location for the next round of GATT (the General Agreements on Tariffs and Trade) talks.

In 1986, the movement re-established itself in Pune, India. Osho died of heart failure in early 1990. His followers claim that he died from complications from being poisoned by the US government while he was in prison in the El Reno Penitentiary in Oklahoma in November 1985. No clear evidence of poisoning was found by doctors who examined him prior to his death. Nevertheless, it is a known fact that thallium is an assassination poison of choice of organizations like the CIA because symptoms of damage appear only after two years, by which time remaining residue of the poison itself cannot be easily found in the victim's body.

Osho is from the East (Clue 1), and his teachings lean towards Tantra, the Eastern religious discipline related Western Hermetic teachings (Clue 2). Tantra also contains the meditative concept of living in the present—the *Now* (see Clue 8). The Osho movement was symbolized in the 1980s by two flying birds; its current symbol is a lone swan flying free from the bonds of Earth and into the cosmos (see Clue 8). Osho was an infuriating traveler to the status quo religions and was thrown out of 21 countries while on his world tour (see Clue 3).

Osho's full legal name—Rajneesh Chandra Mohan—has two connections with *Moon*. "Rajneesh" means "Lord of the Full Moon," and his middle or *second to last name*, "Chandra," means "Moon" (Clue 6).

Although his followers have ceased to wear their red colors in public, their main headquarters at an ashram/meditation resort in India teems with thousands of people wearing robes in shades of maroon (red/rose color: Clues 4 and 5) and Osho even taught them a meditation called "the Mystic *Rose*" there (Clue 4). Despite his death in 1990, Osho's movement continued to flourish: Erich Folath of *Stern* magazine reported in 1993 that attendance at Osho's commune was up by 40 percent from the previous year. In 1995, they reported the biggest increase of attendance ever; interestingly 60 percent never knew the guru while he was alive. The new millennium has witnessed a steady decrease in crowds at the Pune meditation resort; however, there continues to be a surprising upsurge in interest in Osho's books on meditation around the world. Many of his titles are among the hottest sellers in over 30 nations with the Osho International Foundation reporting an average of three million books sold per year, 10 to 15 times more sales then when he was alive. Despite the slight decline in attendance, on average, pilgrims from 110 countries visit his main meditation resort in Pune, India. New generations of seekers are swelling the numbers of the movement, especially through a new interest in Osho generated by Facebook and other social media networks. It clearly has not obtained the level of religious tolerance and outright acceptance that most of the other candidates listed briefly here enjoy. The labels "spiritual rebel" and even "spiritual terrorist" remain associated with this most controversial of twentieth-century mystics as his post-Mortem legacy continues to "infuriate" and "unite" the religions of the world against him.

Osho's links to Nostradamus' eight provided clues seem to match extremely well. We do not know, of course, that the prophet intended his quatrains to imply one religious leader—there could be several: *Many rare birds will cry in the air, 'Now! Now!'*

chapter four

Prophecies
From The Far Distant Future

We now enter the fantastic and metaphorical off-world, interstellar visions of Nostradamus. The light of distant future meaning gleaned from the crowded star field of his familiar phrases and prophetic themes is faint. Indeed, in the following prophecies we may mistake the afterglow of something far more immediate and present day in his message, rather than catch the subtle glimmer of a distant quasar-like prophecy about millennia to come.

They will Live in the Sky
Free From Politics

Si grand Famine par vnde peſtifere,
Par pluye longue le long du polle arctique:
Samarobryn cent lieux de l'hemiſphere,
Viuront ſans loy exempt de pollitique.

**So great a Famine through a pestilent wave.
[It] will extend its rain over the
length of the Arctic pole:
Samarobrin, one hundred leagues
from the hemisphere,
They shall live without law, exempt
from politics.**

6 Q5

The name *Samarobrin* has mystified interpreters of Nostradamus for centuries. According to
the quatrain, whatever Samarobrin is, it is hov-
ering some *hundred leagues* or 270 miles above
us. Modern interpreters have come up with an
intriguing interpretation for this mysterious word:
in Russian, *samo* means "self" and *robrin* means
"operator"; hence, this often used term "self-oper-
ator" by Russian cosmonauts for their space satel-
lites could make Samarobrin stand for either the
Russian space station Mir or today's International
Space Station. Perhaps Nostradamus, when faced
with the images of a space station aloft over the
limb of the Earth, with solar wings outstretched,
could only describe it in terms of the winged
seed pods of elm or maple trees, which are called
samara in Latin. He then added the Latin *obire* to
describe it "orbiting" the Earth.

Samarobrin could be the source of a rare positive prediction from Nostradamus. This quatrain
may imply that scientists aloft in the International

Space Station, working in their zero-gravity space labs, may find a cure for some other future pandemic ravaging the northern hemisphere of Earth. They create new elements in space that cannot be manufactured in gravity on Earth. These inventors shall live *exempt* (or better—*beyond*) mere national law and work to find global solutions 270 miles in orbit above the petty politics of our planet. Or, we can take a broader brush to the cryptic promises of this prophecy and say that Space exploration in the twenty-first century will bring solutions and cures to many of our ills and pestilences whether some third Antichrist triggers them or they arise from the culmination of our anti-conscious behavior. A world seen ever more often from space has no borders and its people are one family.

Finally, Samarobrin could even be Nostradamus' name for an extraterrestrial space craft that orbits Earth in our near future and by its unquestionable existence brings humanity together. The discovery of intelligent life will force us to live intelligently, as such a craft would be proof that others are out there (be they good or evil in intent) and humanity will need to put up a wiser and united front to deal with them.

"Phoning Home" From a Distant World

La nef estrange par le tourment marin,
Abourdera pres de port incogneu:

Nonobſtant ſignes de rameau palmerin,
Apres mort pille bon auis tard venu.

Because of the tormented seas, the strange ship,
Will land at an unknown port:
Notwithstanding the signals from the
branch of palm [radar dish?]
After death, pillage: good birds arriving late.

1 Q30

A strange and alien ship exits the ionic and radio-active solar gales of space to land on an unknown port—a new world. Are they humans come to colonize a new Earth under the stars of a new heaven mentioned later by Nostradamus as those seen from a planet within the constellations of Aquarius, or Cancer? We do not know. A shaft extends from the vehicle that opens the inverted, palm-tree-like array of a communication dish, perhaps in the 30th year of the twenty-first, the twenty-second, or perhaps a year 30 in a century far beyond the next turn of the millennium after 3001 c.e.

The First Intergalactic War?

Les dieux feront aux humains apparence,
Ce qu'ilz feront auteurs de grand conflict:
Auant ciel veu ferain eſpee & lance,
Que vers main gauche fera plus grand afflict.

The gods will make it appear to the humans,
That they will be the authors of a great conflict:
Sword and lance[-like missiles fly] before
heaven [which] is observed as serene,
So that towards the left hand there
will be great affliction.

1 Q91

The next great age of warfare could come on the battlefield of the stars. *The gods* could be an advanced human or alien race responsible for a war in the serene and silent heaven called "Space." These gods may try to hide their responsibility for starting this conflict. Have they hidden the seed of a future showdown in the genetic double helix of the humans they have interbred with eons ago? For a million years, the seed of conflict waited until the day when humans freed themselves from the tether of their little world and entered the vast galactic arena. They contact the "gods" responsible for the theological and mythological fragments that are the foundation of human religions and discover the original deified characters of their myths and scriptures are too frail and human, like themselves, to regard with awe and fear. Indeed the humans to come this far in space to confront their ancestors have become godlike in their own right. Conflict is joined. There is a new battle in heaven between angels. The new

human, space-faring gods of the future crowd
their ancestors off the galactic plane.

Genetically Engineered "Aqua-Humans"

Au Cruftamin par mer Hadriatique,
Apparoiftra vn horrible poiffon:
De face humaine & la fin aquatique,
Qui fe prendra dehors de l'ameçon.

In the Conca by the Adriatic Sea,
There will appear a horrible fish:
With a face [that is] **human and its end aquatic,**
Which will be taken without the hook.

3 Q21

The Conca River drains into the Adriatic ten
miles south of Rimini, the site of Nostradamus'
first vision of the coming human era of multi-
ple species. Enjoy the good old days of a single
human species, for this new twenty-first century
will be the last century to see it. Once human
beings get over their fears of playing god with
genetic engineering, once they begin adapting to
the different gravities and atmospheres of other
worlds in the solar system, and grapple with life
in the weightlessness of space, you will see *Homo
sapiens* branch off into many different species of
human. By the 22nd century, you will think we

have fashioned out of the root *Homo sapiens* species as many variants as earlier geneticists fashioned from breeding thousands of canine "woof" creations from the mother "wolf." We will spawn as many variations of the human species tomorrow as we fashion hundreds of cat and dog variations today. In this prophecy, Nostradamus may describe the human face of a flippered and scale skinned man or woman tailored for life beneath the sea.

A Cosmic Christ is Coming

Le facree pompe viendra baiffer les aifles,
Par la venue du grand legiflateur:
Humble haulfera vexera les rebelles,
Naiftra sur terre aucun æmulateur.

The sacred pomp will come to lower its wings,
At the coming of the great legislator:
He will raise the humble. He will vex the rebels,
None of his like will be born on this Earth.

5 Q79

A distant future interpretation would have this *legislator* be a human born in space or on an extraplanetary colony in our solar system, or a visitor from another star system. Perhaps the one who legislates is the great Messiah of the Aquarian

Age, born in the 25th century, as foreseen by the British palmist and seer Count Louis Hamon in his book *Cheiro's World Predictions* (1931).

Homo angelicus

Le regne humain d'Anglique geniture,
Fera fon regne paix vnion tenir:
Captiue guerre demy de fa clofture,
Long temps la paix leur fera maintenir.

The human realm of Angelic offspring,
Will cause its [his] realm to
hold in peace and union:
War captive halfway inside its [his] enclosure,
For a long time peace will be
maintained by them.

10 Q42

Space-faring humanity will genetically bond with an extraterrestrial humanoid race to take on an appearance that our sixteenth-century prophet can only describe as *angelic* in appearance and nature. This union will eventually bring a lasting peace on Earth—and any new Earths colonized by our distant descendants.

3797 A.D.
The End of the World
And A New Beginning

*...I'ay composéliures de propheties contenāt chacun
cent quatrains aftronomiques de propheties, lefquelles
i'ay vn peu voulu rabouter obfcurement: & font per-
petuelles vaticinations, pour d'icy à l'annee 3797...*

*...Que ie treuue le mōde auāt l'vniuerfelle cōflagra-
tion aduenir tant de deluges & fi hautes inundations, qu'il ne fera guiere terroir qui ne foit couuert
d'eau & fera par fi lōg t˜eps ˜q hors mis enographies
& topographies, que le tout ne foit pery: außi auāt
& apres telles inundatiōs, en plufieurs cōtrees, les
pluyes feront fi exigues, & tōbera du Ciel fi grande
abondāce de feu & de pierre candentes, que n'y demeu-
rera rien qu'il ne foit cōfommé: & cecy aduenir en
brief, & auāt la derniere conflagration. Car encores
que la planette, Mars paracheue fon fiecle, & à la
fin de fon dernier periode fi le reprendra il: mais
affemblez les vns en Aquarius par plufieurs annees,
les autres en Cancer par plus longues & cōtinues.*

**...I have composed books of prophecies, each
containing one hundred astronomical quatrains
composed of prophecies, which I have required**

to polish a little obscurely. They are perpetual prophecies, for they extend from now to the year 3797…

…Before the future universal conflagration [in 3797] the world will see many floods and such high inundations, that there will remain scarcely any land not covered by water, and this will last for so long that outside of the topography of Earth—and the races which inhabit it—everything will perish. Furthermore, before and after these floods many nations shall see very little rain and there will fall from the sky such a great amount of fire and flaming meteors that nothing will remain unconsumed. All this will happen a short time before the final conflagration. For although the planet Mars will finish its cycle, at the end of its last age, [and Mars] will start again. Some will assemble in Aquarius for several years, others in Cancer for a longer time and for evermore.

From the Preface to the
Prophecies of Nostradamus

The date 3797 makes this the most distant dated prediction in history. Nostradamus foresees tremendous gravitational disturbances of a dying Sun making Earth's climate go haywire. These are the first symptoms of the end of the world. Great tidal waves taller than the highest peaks of the continents will roll over Earth's antiquities and ancient-future civilizations. Then a meteor shower of debris from the remains of Venus and Mercury—as the expanding Sun captures them—reduces the surface of our planet to a scorched wasteland. The oceans evaporate and our home planet is consumed.

Astronomers say that the Earth will survive being overcome by the expanding Sun. It will orbit as a white-hot rock in the flames of a red giant (what Nostradamus calls *the final conflagration*). Nostradamus' belief that Mars would continue its orbit outside the Sun might find grudging agreement among astronomers. They believe the aging Sun will have enough mass to expand at—or slightly beyond—the Earth's orbit when it swells into a red giant. Nostradamus and modern astronomers differ on the timing of cosmic doomsday. He believed this would occur 1,797 years after the year 2000. They see it several billion years later.

Even among the embers of this last conflagration, the human race will survive to colonized space. Nostradamus not only reports on the survival of Mars but uses its astrological cycle to define a window of time. In Julian calculation an era of Mars lasts roughly 700 years. With this in mind he is possibly dating the period it takes a number of "arks" to travel the great distances of the galaxy to colonize other star systems.

Tonight, when you step out of your home to behold the vault of the heavens, train your eye upon the distant stars of the constellations of Aquarius and Cancer. There you will see humanity's future home when your descendants will walk upon a new Earth warmed by the sunlight of distant stars. Nostradamus gives some indication that the mission to the stars of Cancer will see humankind build its permanent home. The Old French meaning for *côtinues* (an abbreviation for *continues* in Modern French) gives us "uninterrupted" or *evermore*. Another translation would have our descendants dwelling in worlds around the stars of Cancer *for a longer and uninterrupted time*. Perhaps they will live consciously celebrating the eternity of the present, and therefore live beyond the interruptions of time itself.

Epilogue:

Scared Straight

These visions of space travel, lived in peace and perpetuity—and other prescient promises of the coming of a new religiousness spawned by the appearance of a "Man from the East"—appear in this book with an impact way out of proportion to the general tone of Nostradamus' discourse on the future. Taken in its totality, his tone is the most pessimistic and dark of any prophet who ever lifted the veil of tomorrow. It is an account of murder, tragedy, and violent revolutions. The Bible has but one Antichrist, Nostradamus burdens us with three. If positive futures appear, they seem to do so grudgingly. You can see this fact evident in the quatrain indexing in the Man from the East predictions. They are scattered like lotuses on the muddy floodwaters of ominous auguries of slaughter and sorrows.

Nostradamus nags us about our faults in future tense. It is a shrewish wife's litany of how often we have, and we will, miss our chances to be anything more than robotic, predictable, murderous animals that talk of peace and enlightenment while walking the path of savagery and stupidity.

An Edgar Cayce will sleep-trance his nightmares to us of vast natural disasters and the sinking and rising of continents, but he always balances them with soft and assuring dreams of a Christ-consciousness-driven new humanity to come. Ruth Montgomery's guides frighten us with Axis Shift prophecies set for the end of the twentieth century, but at least they take pity on us when the deadline of doom comes near and toss us another time line of a decade's length. I would add that her spirit guides will be kind enough to keep postponing the tilt of the Earth, with its subsequent thousand mile winds and thousand foot waves destroying civilization, ever to the next decade, and the next, until that eventuality is thrown in the refuse bin of "never-to-happen" where it always belonged. The politically correct prophets will always positively promise a sun-shiny day after the end of days.

Not Nostradamus.

He seems predisposed to view the world as a seer of sour grapes. His view of the future is almost criminal. And that, dear reader, may be why his view of the future is far more profound than that of any other seer.

Who else but a criminal can teach you a lesson of hard love?

I saw such a lesson given once in an award-winning American television documentary entitled

Scared Straight. It concerned a group of American teenage toughs who, upon facing the judge for their petty crimes, were given the choice of going to juvenile jail, or spending an afternoon in the State Penitentiary in an encounter session with a dozen of its worst convicts. In short, the judge was giving these delinquents a chance to see and change their future lives, if they would but listen to the forecasts and confessions of the lifers—the men living in the seventh hell of prison for life.

Guards led the young toughs into the dark and barred halls of the penitentiary through a gauntlet of catcalling, lewd and violent prisoners to sit in a room with the meanest, muscled, scarfaced men in perpetual life-lockdown. The "session" began. An hour later, the cool tough punks exited the room as tearful and vulnerable boys. Eighty percent of those boys would never commit a crime again. The transformation came from just one hour sitting face to face with their future. The convicts had become their Nostradamus, depicting without pity the horrors of what they could expect from a future prison life. There was no let-up to the auguries. They heard of assured rape of pretty, young new prisoners, the mutilation of the body and the deeper mutilation to the soul that comes from the brutality of day-to-day life in prison.

Every time I enter the prophecies of Nostradamus I feel like those boys encountering a man, who out of hard love has seen and understood what is potentially criminal in me, and in you: the destiny of being predictable makes us all passive or active participants in the repeated tragedy of history Nostradamus foretells. The prophet, like the convicts of that prison, does not pull his punches. He rarely gives us hope. His words are full of frightening and violent images of what we have done and "will" do if we remain hell-bent on perpetuating the fundamental crime of every human being. That crime is this: being programmed by society from birth onwards to be predictable, robotic, a dutiful mediocrity and a collector of borrowed personal, national and religious identities. When we are not living from our own truth and experiences, when we allow others to suppress the birthright of natural intelligence and Christ-consciousness in us, then we become delinquent as spiritual beings. Rather than face life with the spontaneity of genius and authenticity we, as children, are forced to follow the paths of the adults who overlord and overwhelm us early on. They do this because the crime was "done" to them. The victims of this criminal conditioning pass it on to the young of our world, just like old prisoners pass on their criminal skills to the new inmates of their world.

I believe Nostradamus saw this repetition of habit as the engine of all that is horrible in our future history. He has applied that pessimism to extremes out of compassion. He is trying to scare us straight. He used fire to put out fire, as it were.

Rather than give us condolences and hope, he scares us with the crimes of the future, the wars and the devastations. By painting a future so dire he is like those brutal convicts breathing down on our delinquent dreams that all will turn out good in the end because someone else—not you or me—will wake up in time and change the future's course for the better. You can hold that idea, and think you are pretty cool and aware until you enter his prophecies and see him rave and rant therein. You will soon find out that you and your future are not that cool, and you know nothing about being tough. You will see from his litany of prophecies fulfilled and prophecies to come that you are a part of the crime of habit that plants the seeds of tomorrow's wars and tragedies in every new generation. You are today's criminal teaching your children to be criminals tomorrow and Nostradamus, a prisoner of pessimistic prophecy for life, is trying to scare *you* straight out of that habit.

Once you come out of his chamber of horrors into the sunlight, take his lesson to heart and to soul.

Change.

THE END
(11 September 2014)

OTHER BOOKS BY JOHN HOGUE

A NEW COLD WAR
The Prophecies of Nostradamus, Stormberger and Edgar Cayce

Prophets, such as Nostradamus, Stormberger, and others introduced in this new and topical book accurately dated, detailed and forecast the coming of the First, the Second, and perhaps a "Third" World War. A new cold war between America and Russia "in our future" would merely be a short prelude to the threat of a civilization-ending nuclear exchange that no one saw coming.

With open eyes, we "walk into these great catastrophes," so the prophets say.

The future has another destiny. Edgar Cayce foresaw Russia becoming the "Hope of the World" with the help and support of American friendship. From citing future dangers to offering solutions, these prophets might show us the way to lasting peace.

—⫘—

NOSTRADAMUS
The End of End Times

Read John Hogue's last—and often satirical—word on Mayan doomsday or "bloomsday" and first word on the many other significant and ongoing reboots of prophetic time cycles that a fawning paparazzi obsession with the Mayan Calendar had overlooked and neglected while they are still transforming human destiny.

—⫘—

NOSTRADAMUS AND
THE ANTICHRIST
Code Named Mabus

Explore clues to unlock the true identity of the man of evil, code named *Mabus,* the third and final Antichrist foreseen by the world-renowned sixteenth-century prophet. John Hogue plays prophetic detective presenting his evidence after a 25-year search lining up contemporary candidates whose names and actions may implicate one of them as the man who would ignite a world war.

—⫘—

NOSTRADAMUS: THE WAR WITH IRAN
Islamic Prophecies of the Apocalypse

Never has Nostradamus "come into the clear" like this, naming names, accurately dating events and places outright about a war in the Persian Gulf between America and Israel against Iran. Ships will be "melted and sunk by the Trident"! Is he speaking of US trident nuclear missiles, or, the mysterious trident symbol hidden in the Iranian flag? This war is dated to happen after an interlude of peace negotiations in 2014 lead to the worst region-wide conflict the Middle East has ever seen. Armageddon, perhaps? That depends on accessing Nostradamus' alternative future hidden in prophecies written over 450 years ago. Peace is possible, dated for the last dark hour before a war that will change the life of every human being.

—⁂—

NOSTRADAMUS
A Life and Myth

John Hogue published the first full-bodied biography of one of the most famous and controversial historical figures of the last millennium. He traces the life and legacy of the French prophet in fascinating and insightful detail, revealing much little known and original material never before published in English.

—ɱ—

KAMIKAZE TOMORROWLAND
A Future Fiction Story

Akio Sarazawa, a Kamikaze pilot, dives his bomb laden fighter 90 degrees through a gauntlet of anti-aircraft fire. His target is the rectangular mass of a US Carrier swerving through the Pacific to avoid his crash. Maneuver as it might, it can't escape. The flight deck rising rapidly before him floats on a wall of ocean, beckoning, as if it is a doorway. But moments before the pilot meets this portal out of life, he thinks how good it would be not see the future death of his homeland. He is wrong. A devil's sea has other shocking, touching and altogether absurd surprises waiting on the other side.

ABOUT THE AUTHOR

Author of 26 books in 19 languages, "Rogue" scholar, world-renowned authority on Nostradamus and the prophetic traditions of the world. Please visit him at www.hogueprophecy.com

Made in the USA
San Bernardino, CA
25 September 2016